WORLD BOOK'S

YOUNG SCIENTIST

WORLD BOOK'S

YOUNG SCIENTIST

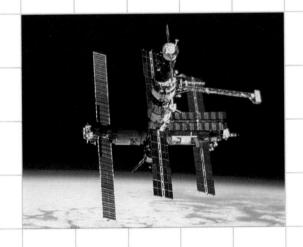

- COMMUNICATION
- ENERGY

8

World Book, Inc.
a Scott Fetzer company
Chicago

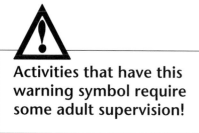

Activities that have this warning symbol require some adult supervision!

The quest to explore the known world and to describe its creation and subsequent development is nearly as old as mankind. In the Western world, the best-known creation story comes from the book of Genesis. It tells how God created Earth and all living things. Modern religious thinkers interpret the Biblical story of creation in various ways. Some believe that creation occurred exactly as Genesis describes it. Others think that God's method of creation is revealed through scientific investigation. *Young Scientist* presents an exciting picture of what scientists have learned about life and the universe.

World Book, Inc.
233 N. Michigan Avenue
Chicago, IL 60601

For information on other World Book products, call 1-800-WORLDBK (967-5325), or visit us at our Web site at http://www.worldbook.com

© 1997, 1995, 1991, 1990 World Book, Inc.

ISBN: 0-7166-2758-2 (volume VIII)
ISBN: 0-7166-2797-3 (set)

Library of Congress Catalog Card No. 00-107193

Printed in the United States of America

1 2 3 4 5 6 7 06 05 04 03 02 01 00

Contents

Communication

Energy

COMMUNICATION

Exchanging messages

Every minute of every day, all over the world, people are sending messages to one another. Just think of the number of different ways you can receive messages in your own home. Your radio and television deliver messages in the form of programs, and your cassette player and videocassette recorder (VCR) allow you to record the programs and play them back later. When you talk on the telephone, you are sending and receiving messages.

Getting the message

Sending and receiving messages is called **communicating**. People communicate with one another in many different ways. They can speak to one another, make gestures with their hands or faces, or even write a note. It is easy to communicate with someone who is in the same room with you, but more difficult if that person is a mile away. In the past, people have sent messages over long distances by using drums, flashing lights, or smoke signals.

Talking with electricity

One hundred and fifty years ago, people would have been amazed if they had known that we would talk to people thousands of miles away, receive pictures in our own homes from space, and send instant copies of letters or photographs from one place to another.

Today, modern systems are very rapid and reliable. We use electricity to send and receive messages by telephone, answering machine, facsimile, modem, radio, and television. This method of exchanging messages is called **telecommunications.** It all began with the invention of the electric telegraph. The electric telegraph marked the beginning of the telecommunications age that we live in today.

Telecommunications has made it possible for people to communicate in split seconds over long distances.

Lung power

We talk, sing, or shout so that other people can hear us. But how does the sound we make reach them? The sound of our voices travels through the air as **waves.** Sound waves are tiny movements of air called **vibrations.** You can feel these vibrations if you shout close to a piece of paper placed on your hand. The sound waves hit the paper and make it vibrate. As vibrations spread out and move away from us, they gradually become weaker and fainter.

Catch those sound waves

Find out how to throw your voice and catch sound.

You will need:

2 triangles of stiff cardboard

a stone or pebble

scissors

masking tape

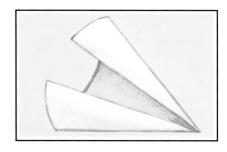

1. Make a megaphone by folding one corner of the cardboard across to the other. Curve the cardboard around so that two sides meet and make a cone.

2. Tape the edges together. Snip off the point to make a hole. Now make another cone exactly the same way to use as an ear trumpet.

3. Go to a park or open space with a friend. Stand facing each other but quite far apart. Then shout out something to your friend. If your friend can hear you, he or she should step back. Keep doing this until your friend can no longer hear you. Mark this spot with a stone.

Traveling sound

If you shout louder, the sound waves you make will be louder and will travel farther. But even the loudest sound soon dies away. A simple instrument like a megaphone can make sound travel farther because it directs the sound waves and keeps them from spreading out so much. An ear trumpet enables you to hear sounds better. Its funnel shape collects the sound waves so that they become stronger. Why do cheerleaders use megaphones?

4. Now try it again. This time, ask your friend to cup both hands behind the ears. How far from the stone is your friend?

sound waves

5. Now try shouting through your megaphone. Does this carry your voice even farther?

6. Ask your friend to use the ear trumpet. What difference does this make?

sound waves

Find out more by looking
at pages **16–17**
　　　　　　36–37

Pass the message

If you receive a message and pass it on to someone else, you are acting as a **relay.** Relays are useful for sending messages over long distances.

In telecommunications, electronic relays pick up a signal and make it stronger before passing it on. Without relays, the signal would be too weak to understand by the time it reached the end of its journey.

Pony Express

One of the most famous relay systems was the Pony Express, which carried mail from St. Joseph, Missouri, over the mountains to Sacramento, California. This was in 1860 and 1861, before there were railways or telegraph lines across North America. Pony Express riders used fast horses or ponies. The horses were changed every 10 to 15 miles (16 to 24 kilometers). Each rider traveled 74 miles (120 kilometers) or more in a working day. So a message got through much more quickly than it would have with a single messenger. But by October 1861, the transcontinental telegraph was completed, and the Pony Express was no longer needed.

Riders of the Pony Express traveled in relays day and night in all kinds of weather. A package could travel the entire 1,962-mile (3,164-kilometer) trail in 10 days or less.

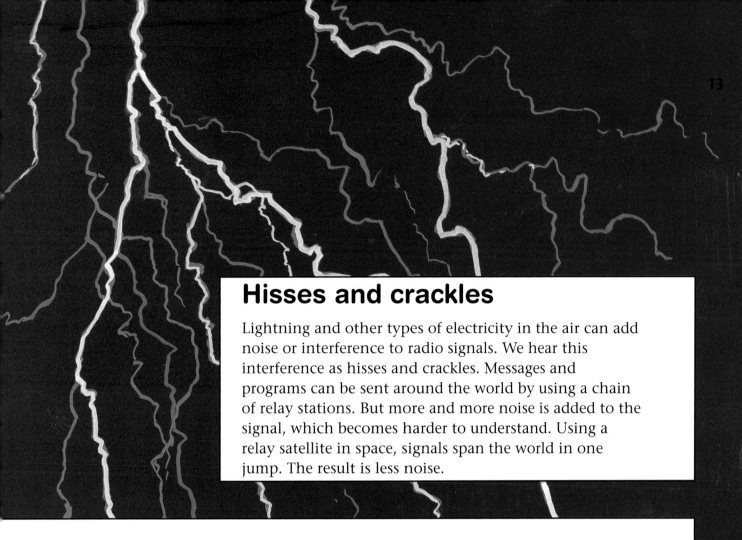

Hisses and crackles

Lightning and other types of electricity in the air can add noise or interference to radio signals. We hear this interference as hisses and crackles. Messages and programs can be sent around the world by using a chain of relay stations. But more and more noise is added to the signal, which becomes harder to understand. Using a relay satellite in space, signals span the world in one jump. The result is less noise.

The relay game

Playing the relay game shows how easy it is for relayed messages to be changed or misunderstood.

Make up a group of eight or more people in a circle. One person whispers a 10-word message to the next person, who whispers it on, and so on around the circle. No one may whisper the message more than once.

When the message has gone around the circle, the last person calls it out. The person who started calls out the original message.

You can make the game more difficult by sending two messages in opposite directions at the same time.

Signaling

Throughout history, armies and navies have sent messages across battlefields. Simple orders like "Advance" or "Retreat" could be given by bugle calls or cannon fire. But sending reports of the battle back to headquarters needed a different system.

Semaphore

During the 1790's, a Frenchman named Claude Chappe invented a signaling system called **semaphore**. Semaphore is a system of sending signals by means of two jointed arms at the tops of tall posts. These arms could be moved to different positions to show different letters of the alphabet. Each semaphore station was built on a hill so that it could be seen, using a telescope, from the next station in any direction. In this way, messages could be relayed over long distances from one station to the next. Semaphore stations on the coast would send messages to ships at sea.

Signal for battle

On the battlefield, there might not be a semaphore station, but messages could be sent by stationing signalers with large flags on nearby hills. They used the same code as the semaphore arms. An expert signaler could send or receive up to 25 letters a minute, and messages could be relayed nearly 155 miles (250 kilometers) in 15 minutes.

A semaphore signaler holds two flags in different positions for each letter of the alphabet. The signaler can also communicate other signals, such as words, phrases, and numbers.

A   B   C   D   E   F   G   H   I   J   K

R   S   T   U   V   W   X   Y

Signals at sea

Sailors signaled to one another with flags. The picture shows one of the most famous naval signals in British history. It was sent by Admiral Lord Nelson to the British fleet before the Battle of Trafalgar, in 1805. It read "England expects every man will do his duty."

England   expects   every   man   will   do   his   D   U   T   Y

Semaphore was also called the aerial telegraph. Many hills where semaphore stations were built are still called Telegraph Hill.

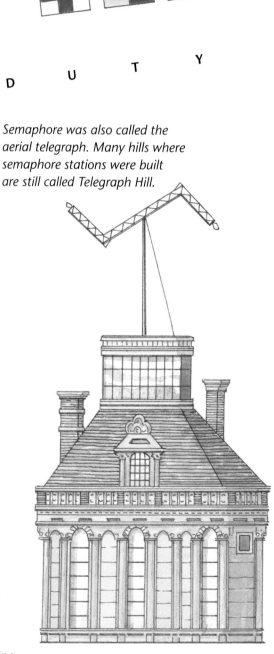

L   M   N   O   P   Q

Z   Error   End of word   Numbers follow   Attention   Answering sign

Dots and dashes

In 1832, an American artist sailed home from Europe. He had spent some time painting in Europe and hoped to sell his paintings when he arrived home. His name was Samuel Morse.

Talking through wires

The journey on the ship was to change Samuel Morse's life. He met a young chemist from Boston named Charles Jackson, who showed him how an electromagnet works. Morse became interested in electricity and in the idea of sending messages along electric wires. Morse was one of the first people to make an **electric telegraph.** An electric telegraph uses an electric current to send messages along a wire.

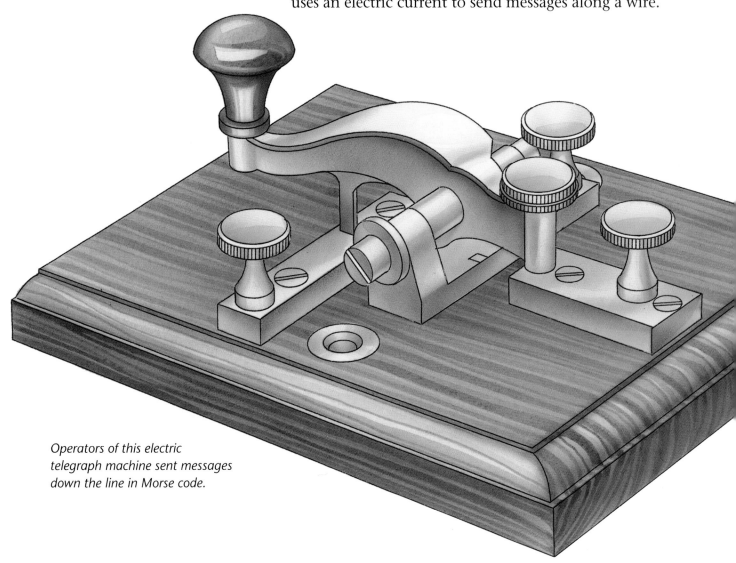

Operators of this electric telegraph machine sent messages down the line in Morse code.

A ● ━
B ━ ● ● ●
C ━ ● ━ ●
D ━ ● ●
E ●
F ● ● ━ ●
G ━ ━ ●
H ● ● ● ●
I ● ●
J ● ━ ━ ━
K ━ ● ━
L ● ━ ● ●
M ━ ━
N ━ ●
O ━ ━ ━
P ● ━ ━ ●
Q ━ ━ ● ━
R ● ━ ●
S ● ● ●
T ━
U ● ● ━
V ● ● ● ━
W ● ━ ━
X ━ ● ● ━
Y ━ ● ━ ━
Z ━ ━ ● ●

1 ● ━ ━ ━ ━
2 ● ● ━ ━ ━
3 ● ● ● ━ ━
4 ● ● ● ● ━
5 ● ● ● ● ●
6 ━ ● ● ● ●
7 ━ ━ ● ● ●
8 ━ ━ ━ ● ●
9 ━ ━ ━ ━ ●
0 ━ ━ ━ ━ ━

Morse code

It was a code, not a telegraph that made Morse famous. He gave his name to the code of dots and dashes that he invented. Until this time, most long-distance messages were sent by semaphore. The problem with the electric telegraph was that an electric current can be arranged in only two ways. Either the current is flowing and is "on," or it is "off." Somehow a way had to be found of using the flow of current to make a code that could be sent along the wires.

Morse's answer was to make codes for different letters and numbers out of short and long bursts, or **pulses**, of electric current. He called these **dots** and **dashes**. Using dots and dashes in different orders made the different codes. The Morse "key" that makes the pulses is a kind of switch that turns the current on and off. Messages sent by electric telegraph were marked by the receiving machine on a moving strip of paper. Then the telegraph operator decoded the dots and dashes into ordinary letters and numbers. But operators who used Morse code soon became skilled at decoding the messages directly by listening to the clicks made by the machine. The **international**, or **continental**, **Morse code** is shown opposite.

The emergency signal in Morse code, SOS, is known to sailors all over the world. They use it to call for urgent help if a ship is in danger.

● ● ● ━ ━ ━ ● ● ●

Morse invented a different dot-and-dash pattern for each letter and number.

Communicating by light

Sometimes when you are in open country, you may catch a flash of sunlight on the windshield of a car many miles away. The windshield acts like a mirror and reflects the light. You have probably shone a flashlight beam against a wall or ceiling and watched the spot of light. Cover the mirror or flashlight with your hand, and the light disappears.

Heliograph

Put these two ideas together, and you have one of the oldest ways of communicating in the world—signaling by the light of the sun. The ancient Greeks signaled to each other in this way. They used an instrument called a **heliograph.** The name comes from the ancient Greek words for "sun" and "writing." On a clear day, a heliograph could be seen up to 30 miles (48 kilometers) away without a telescope.

The modern heliograph is mounted on a tripod, like a camera. It can turn in any direction. The mirror flashes when it is directed at the sun and can then be dipped away or covered with a shutter. If the signaler wants to send a message in a direction away from the sun, a second mirror is used to reflect light on to the first. Heliograph messages are sent in Morse code.

You can send heliograph messages using a simple mirror. Tilt the mirror so that it catches the sun's rays. Then reflect the rays toward your friend.

Messages in the dark

A heliograph can be used only in the daytime when the sun is shining. But at night, light messages can be sent using a powerful searchlight called an Aldis lamp. It has a shutter that can be moved to block out the light and also make the dots and dashes of Morse code.

The Aldis lamp has a shutter that breaks up the light into Morse dots and dashes.

At night, lighthouses flash codes of light to warn ships away from a dangerous coastline.

Messages over the wire

The first electric telegraph systems were patented in England in 1837 and in the United States in 1840. The first **telegram**, or message sent by telegraph, was sent in England in 1843. By the 1860's, most of the large cities in Europe and in North America were linked by telegraph. For the first time, people could exchange messages almost instantly over long distances. The telegraph could be used day or night in any kind of weather. The operator also could send a message to a number of different places at the same time.

The key and the sounder

The two parts of the telegraph are the key, which is used to send a message, and the sounder, which receives it. Pressing down on the key completes a circuit and allows an electric current to be sent over the wire. When the current reaches the sounder, it flows through a magnet and attracts an iron bar, which makes a click as it hits the magnet. The patter or the clicking noise is the Morse code.

With the telegraph, people could exchange messages almost instantly over long distances.

Be a telegraph operator

See how well you and a friend would do as telegraph operators. Using the Morse code list on page 17, write out a message in Morse code. Tap out the message using a spoon or knife on a pot or pan. Use slow taps for dashes and shorter taps for dots. Be sure to pause after every letter and leave a slightly longer pause at the end of each word.

Your friend will listen to the patterns of slow and fast taps and write out the message in Morse code, using dashes and dots and drawing a vertical line at the end of each letter or word. Then your friend will use the Morse code table to translate your message.

When your message has been translated, switch places and let your friend send you a message for you to translate.

You will need:

spoon

pot or pan

pencil or pen

paper

Faster printed messages

As telegraph lines began to link towns and cities, people realized that the telegraph could be used to transmit many different kinds of information. Newspaper reporters used the telegraph to send news stories across North America. Financial services used the telegraph to send money orders and exchange information about stock prices. Soon, engineers and inventors had to look for ways to increase the speed at which signals could be handled. They invented a machine that recorded messages in code as a series of holes punched into a paper tape. The machine then sent the message at high speeds. A similar machine received the message and then printed it out in Morse code.

Telegraph machines could send only one message in one direction at a time. In 1872, a system was developed that could send two messages, one in each direction, at the same time. A few years later, new telegraph systems could handle four and five messages at the same time.

In the first half of the last century, financial services used the telegraph to send money orders and exchange information about stock prices, right. Today, stock prices are transmitted and displayed electronically, opposite page.

Teletypewriter and telephoto

Engineers linked a typewriter keyboard, a telegraph machine, and a printer to create the **teletypewriter**, sometimes called a **teleprinter**. The operator sat at an electromechanical typewriter and typed in the message. Each key sent a different electric signal over the wires to the receiving machine, which printed the message. In the 1950's, news services began sending stories to newspapers using teletypewriters. A modern teletypewriter exchange service, called **Telex**, allowed businesses to have teletypewriters in their own offices. Telex is still in use by some businesses.

The telephoto machine allowed news services to send pictures to newspapers over the telephone wire. A scanning device scanned the picture and changed the image into electric signals. A printer at the other end changed the signals back into an image and printed the picture. Newspapers and news services send photos using modern satellite communications.

The fax machine

Today, when people want to send words and images instantly, they often use a **facsimile**, or **fax**, machine. A fax machine uses an electronic scanner to change a printed image into a pattern of tiny dots. This pattern is turned into electrical signals that are sent over the telephone line. The receiving fax machine converts the signal pattern and prints it out onto special paper. The result is a facsimile, or copy, of the original image.

Newspapers used teletypewriters to send and receive news from all over the world. Most modern offices now use fax machines to send and receive messages and pictures.

How the telephone works

More than 100 years ago, a Scottish-born inventor and educator named Alexander Graham Bell was sure that electricity could be used to carry voices over long distances. But how could the sound of voices be turned into electricity? Eventually, after many years of hard work, Bell found the answer. His invention was the first kind of **telephone.** It completely changed people's lives. Telephones have improved tremendously since Bell's time. For example, have you spoken to someone very far away on the telephone? It's amazing how clear the person's voice is—even from the other side of the world.

Voices, like other sounds, make vibrations in the air called **sound waves.** Sound waves are different from one another. Some are loud, some are soft, and some vibrate much more quickly than others. This means that each sound wave can be turned into an electric signal, which can travel along a wire.

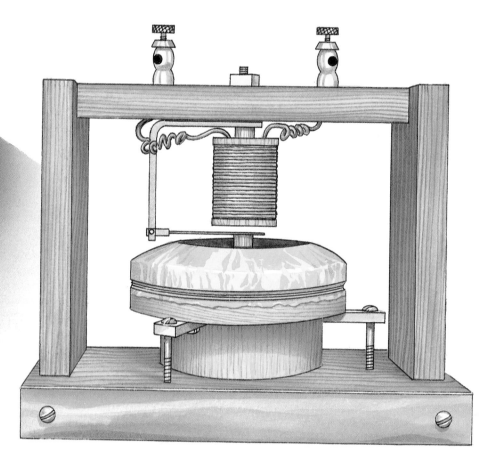

This is the first telephone, invented by Alexander Graham Bell in 1876. The first one-way, long-distance call was made in Ontario, Canada, between two towns 8 miles (13 kilometers) apart.

What's inside the telephone?

When you speak into the telephone, the sound waves of your voice cause a disk called a **diaphragm** to vibrate at various speeds. As the diaphragm moves in one direction, it pushes carbon granules placed behind it closer together. This allows an electric current to pass through the carbon granules easily. As the diaphragm moves in the opposite direction, the electric current becomes weaker. These changes in the electric current happen very quickly as your voice vibrates the diaphragm. The current flows along a telephone wire to the earpiece of another telephone.

In the receiving telephone, an electromagnet pulls a diaphragm in the earpiece. As the electric current becomes stronger or weaker, the diaphragm moves in or out. This movement makes the air vibrate to produce sound waves that duplicate your voice, which the listener hears.

The earpiece of the telephone contains a thin, round metal disk called a diaphragm. Behind the diaphragm is an electromagnet, which behaves like a magnet when an electric current flows through it.

diaphragm

electromagnet

permanent magnet

The mouthpiece of the telephone contains a microphone. The microphone has a thin metal disk or diaphragm. Behind the disk are carbon granules, which allow an electric current to flow.

diaphragm

Connecting your call

There are millions of telephones in the world. Each one can be connected with any of the others. Each telephone in a town or district is joined by wires to the local telephone exchange. The telephone exchanges in different towns or districts are linked by more wires or by trunk cables. Over longer distances, radio transmitters and receivers, or even satellites, transmit signals.

Dialing a number

Every home or office has its own phone number. Dialing a number causes an electric signal to travel along the telephone wire. The signal makes a connection to a telephone at the number dialed. **Touch-tone telephones** use a pair of musical tones to create the signal. Each pair of tones stands for a different number on the telephone. The tones tell the telephone company's computers exactly where to direct the call. Older **rotary telephones** used a dial with one finger hole for each number. Dialing the number sent a certain number of electric pulses over the line. For example, dialing "7" caused the telephone to send out seven pulses.

After you've dialed the phone, the signals travel over the line to the local telephone exchange. Inside the telephone exchange, switchgear connects the many thousands of calls that pass through the exchange every day.

Find out more by looking
at pages 24–25
28–29
32–33

Putting you through

When the electric signals reach the telephone exchange,
automatic switches send more electric signals over the lines
to the number you dialed. When the telephone rings at the
other end, the person who answers it picks up the handset,
or receiver, as it is usually called. This automatically stops the
telephone from ringing, and the conversation can begin.
Your words are then transmitted over the line by another set
of electric signals.

By land, sea, or air

International and other long-distance calls may pass through
many exchanges before the final connection is made. The
signals can travel from one exchange to the next by land
line, underwater cable, or by satellite. Radio relay systems use
short radio waves called **microwaves.** Microwaves can be
beamed directly between the exchanges. Or they may go
through a communications satellite in orbit thousands of
miles above Earth.

telephone exchange

telephone exchange

telephone exchange

Find out more by looking at pages **26–27**

Sharing the line

Just suppose that one million people in one city wanted to speak to one million people in another city—all at the same time. Then one million wires or radio links would be needed to join them. There simply isn't room for all these wires or radio stations. Instead, the links between the telephone exchanges are shared, which means that fewer wires or radio links are needed.

Long-distance call

When you talk over a long distance, you share your link with many other people. You cannot hear their conversations because each conversation is carried on a different frequency (rate of vibration). This means that many conversations use one wire or a single radio link, but they do not interfere with one another.

The line between these two telephone exchanges is shared among the red, yellow, and blue callers. Follow each color from the caller, through the two exchanges, and to the correct receiver.

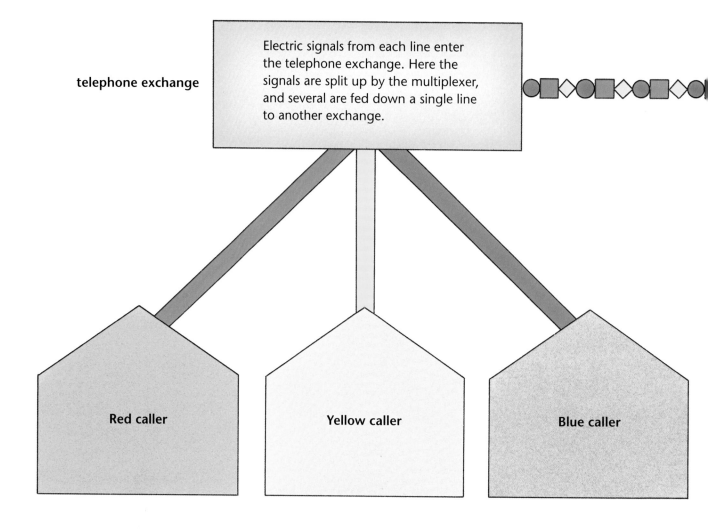

telephone exchange

Electric signals from each line enter the telephone exchange. Here the signals are split up by the multiplexer, and several are fed down a single line to another exchange.

Red caller

Yellow caller

Blue caller

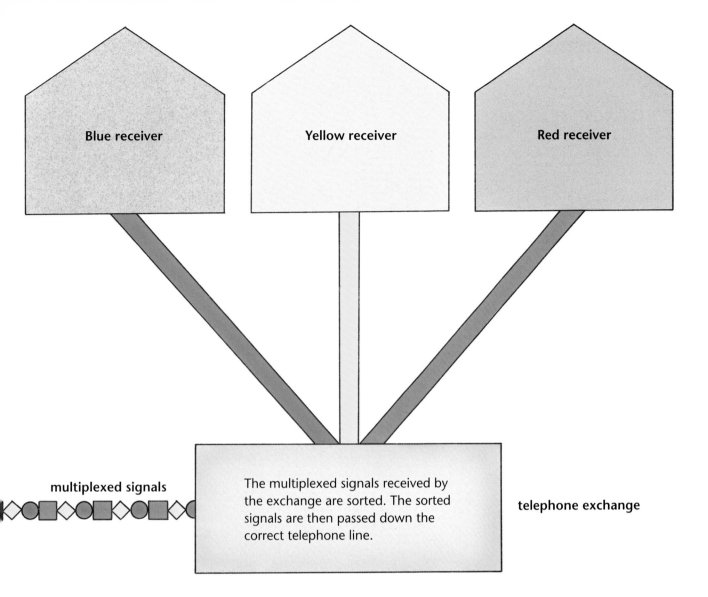

Blue receiver

Yellow receiver

Red receiver

multiplexed signals

The multiplexed signals received by the exchange are sorted. The sorted signals are then passed down the correct telephone line.

telephone exchange

Coding your call

When you speak into your telephone, the vibrations made by your voice are turned into varied electric currents. These electric currents—the signals—travel over the wire. At the exchange, the vibrating electric signals are turned into a code. The coded electric signals are not vibrating, but they are a string of pulses. It is like turning a switch on and off very quickly. The coded signals from different conversations are divided up into pieces by a **multiplexer.** These pieces are then sent one after the other through the wire or radio link between exchanges.

At the receiving exchange, the pieces are sorted out and put back together again by another multiplexer. Each complete coded signal is then decoded and sent over the line to the person you are calling. What you hear is the voice of your friend as clearly as if that person were nearby.

The string telephone

A string telephone does not need electricity to make it work. It works by changing the sound of your voice into vibrations, which travel along the string. When they reach the other end, the vibrations are changed back into sound again.

You will need:

two or three empty plastic cups

a ball of thin, strong string

Over and out

When you use the string telephone, you will have to figure out a way of telling the person at the other end when to listen and when to speak. One way is to copy the system that radio operators use. When you have finished speaking and are ready for an answer, you say "Over." This is the signal for the person at the other end to speak. When you come to the end of the conversation, you say "Out."

If there are three of you, you can make a third string telephone and use it as an extension. Tie the string to the first line in a convenient place.

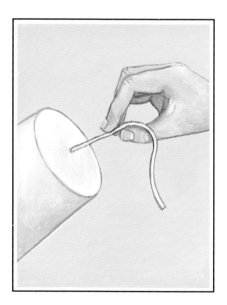

1. Make a small hole in the end of each plastic cup and thread an end of the string through the hole.

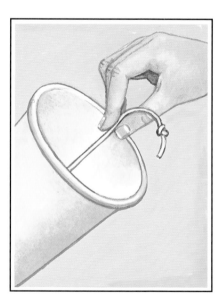

2. Tie a knot on the inside to keep it in place. The plastic cup acts as both mouthpiece and earpiece.

Find out more by looking at pages **24–25**

Connect three string phones. Then, you and two friends can all take part in a fun phone conversation.

3. If you make sure that the string is stretched tight, you can use the string telephone to talk to someone in another part of the room.

The bottom of the cup acts like a diaphragm. Your voice causes it to vibrate. The vibrations pass along the string and cause the bottom of the listener's cup to vibrate. The vibrations are then changed back into the same set of sounds that you spoke.

The string must be kept tight. If the string is loose, the vibrations from your voice are lost into the air. If it is tight, they cannot escape easily and so move down the string to the other end.

Find out more by looking at pages **26–27**

Wires under the sea

You may have watched workers digging up the streets of your town to repair electric cables. You have probably seen telephone and telegraph wires strung between pylons or poles from city to city. But how can people communicate from one continent to another? One way is to send messages along long cables sunk under the ocean floor.

Laying cables

It sounds easy to unroll a giant reel of insulated cable into the sea, letting it sink to the seabed. But the first engineers to lay underwater cables soon discovered all kinds of problems. Rocks on the seabed damage the insulation. The cable can easily break when it is being laid. Once in place, it can be damaged by ships' anchors, fishing nets, or sea creatures.

The British steamship S.S. Great Eastern *laid the first successful transatlantic cable in 1866. The cable stretched from Ireland to Newfoundland in Canada.*

Seabed Tractor and SCARAB

Engineers use remote-controlled underwater vehicles to lay undersea cable and repair it when it breaks. Crews on board ships on the surface operate these vehicles. One of these vehicles, called Seabed Tractor, drives along the seabed, using water jets, a mechanical claw, or a rock cutter to dig a trench about 3 feet (1 meter) deep. Five video cameras help keep it on course. Another underwater vehicle, called SCARAB, can find breaks in undersea cable. After SCARAB finds the break, the repair ship pulls up the cable and fixes it. SCARAB then digs a trench using water jets and reburies the cable under the sea floor.

A SCARAB is a remote-controlled underwater vehicle that finds breaks in undersea cable. It reburies the cable after the repair ship fixes it.

Messages on waves

Messages can be sent over long distances by telegraph and telephone. Until the late 1800's, long-distance messages had to be relayed by wire. Then scientists discovered **radio waves.** Radio waves can travel through empty space.

In 1895, Guglielmo Marconi, an Italian scientist, became the first person to send radio signals through the air. At first, radio messages were sent in Morse code. Experimental radio broadcasts began about 1910.

Vibrating signals

Radio waves are electric signals that vibrate millions of times a second as they travel. Radio waves travel at a speed of 186,282 miles (299,792 kilometers) per second—that's the speed of light.

Radio waves are described according to their **frequency** and their **amplitude.** Frequency depends on wavelength. For example, some radio waves, called high-frequency waves, have a short wavelength. This means that the distance from the crest of one wave to the crest of the next is short. Low-frequency waves have longer wavelengths. Amplitude, a measure of a radio wave's strength, is the distance from its crest to its trough.

You cannot see or hear radio waves, but there are many different radio waves traveling between transmitters and receivers.

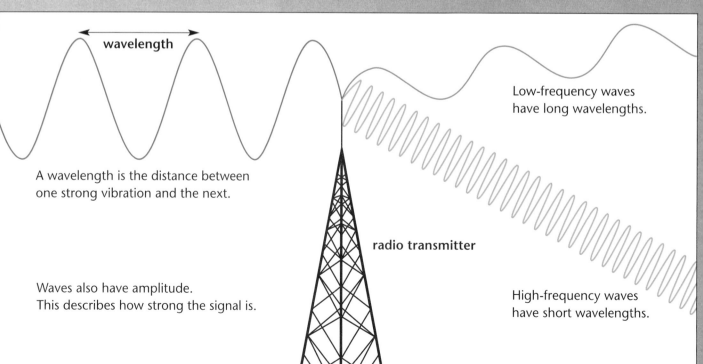

wavelength

A wavelength is the distance between one strong vibration and the next.

Waves also have amplitude.
This describes how strong the signal is.

radio transmitter

Low-frequency waves have long wavelengths.

High-frequency waves have short wavelengths.

A radio transmitter can send radio waves into space, where satellites can beam them back to a receiving station on Earth.

Radio broadcast

When radio waves are broadcast, they travel over different distances. Some waves, called **ground waves**, travel parallel to Earth's surface, trapped between the ground and a layer of the atmosphere called the **ionosphere**. Another type of wave, called a **sky wave**, bounces back off the ionosphere. Other waves, called UHF and VHF, can travel through the ionosphere and be relayed by satellite.

satellite

Sky waves can travel over long distances. They do this by bouncing off the ionosphere.

Ground waves travel parallel to Earth's surface. Ground waves are trapped between the surface of Earth and the ionosphere.

ionosphere

Earth

UHF and VHF waves travel in straight lines as far as the horizon. But if they are directed toward the sky, they can travel through the ionosphere. Satellites in space can direct the waves back to Earth.

Medium waves also follow Earth's surface but do not travel as far as ground waves.

36

Find out more by looking
at pages **26–27**
       50–51

More about radio waves

In its early days, radio was called "wireless." Unlike the telegraph and the telephone, it did not need wires to send messages. Radio signals can travel almost anywhere—even through space. But how does radio work? A radio station has a **transmitter** connected to an **antenna.** The transmitter creates a radio signal, which the antenna sends out. The main part of the radio signal is called the **carrier wave.** It is like an empty, invisible road between the station and your radio.

Transmitting signals

When the station broadcasts a program, it changes the music or speech sounds into electric signals and sends them out on the carrier wave. A radio **receiver** "separates" the signals from the carrier and turns them back into sounds.

Try throwing a pebble into the middle of a pond. The splash sends waves toward the edge. These water waves are like a carrier wave. If you throw a second pebble into the pond, the second splash changes the pattern of waves created by the first pebble. In the same way, the electric signals made from sounds being broadcast change the pattern of the carrier wave.

broadcasting studio

In the broadcasting studio, the speaker's voice is turned into electric signals. These are passed on to a transmitter. There, the signals are added to a carrier wave before being sent over the air.

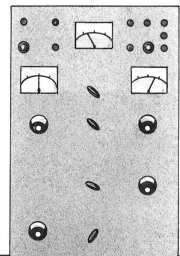

transmitter

antenna

Altering the carrier wave

When the carrier wave is carrying these electric signals, it is known as a modulated carrier. The M in AM and FM stands for "modulation." Since many radios are able to pick up AM and FM broadcasting, the controls of these radios are labeled "AM" and "FM."

AM picks up broadcasts on the short, medium, or long wavebands of a radio. These broadcasts are known as amplitude modulation (AM), because they alter the strength of the carrier wave.

Frequency modulation (FM) works on a very high frequency waveband (VHF) and changes the frequency of the wave.

Radio waves are sent out from the transmitter and are picked up by the radio antenna.

Tuning in

If you switch on the radio and turn the tuning knob or press the digital tuner, you can hear programs from many different stations. Some are local programs, broadcast only in the area where you live. Others are national, broadcast all over the country. Some may come from other countries. Others are broadcast throughout the world. With so many radio programs, how does your radio find the one you have chosen?

The radio **antenna** picks up all the available signals in all the **wavebands.** The listener uses a switch or button on the radio to select a range of frequencies, called a waveband, for the radio to focus on. Radio wavebands are divided into long, medium, and short wavebands. The listener then uses the **tuner** to choose a frequency.

This radio can pick up long-wave, medium-wave, and short-wave signals, as well as AM and FM frequencies. The number shown on the dial is the frequency being received. Buttons marked with arrows allow the listener to scan for strong signals. Buttons below the dial allow the listener to choose a particular waveband.

When a radio is tuned to the medium waveband, for example, it picks up only medium-wave signals. These pass into the radio through the antenna. All the signals, except the chosen one, pass through the radio unheard.

Some car radios have "pre-set" tuning. The driver presses a button which sets the station to a pre-selected station. Some car radios also have a scan feature that finds the station giving the strongest and clearest signal. These features allow the driver to concentrate on driving while finding a program.

Choosing your program

Suppose someone wants to listen to a program on the medium waveband. The listener presses a switch or turns a knob to tune the radio to the medium waveband. Now the radio will pick up only those stations that are transmitting on this waveband.

Each radio station transmits on its own wavelength. If a listener wants to hear a station transmitting on a wavelength of 1,000 feet (300 meters), he or she turns the tuning knob or presses the digital tuner so that 1,000 (300) is marked on the dial. This changes the current flowing inside the radio so that it sorts out radio waves of the chosen length. All the other radio signals pass through the radio unheard.

Some digital radios have "pre-set" tuning. This means that a listener can set the radio to receive signals on a number of different wavelengths and then choose the desired program by pressing a button. This is particularly useful on car radios. The driver can find a program and still concentrate on driving.

Another type of radio can scan, or hunt through, the wavelengths until it finds the station giving the strongest and clearest signal. This feature is useful for people seeking short-wave broadcasts from other countries.

Strengthening the signal

As radio waves travel away from the transmitter, they grow weaker. If the signals they carry are to be changed into sounds inside your radio, they have to be made stronger again once they reach the radio. There are two reasons why radio signals need to be strong and clear. First, they have to be quite strong to make the radio's speaker or headphones work. The second reason is that there is always electrical interference in the air. Unless the signals are clear and strong, this interference can cause an annoying background noise.

The amplifier

The part of the radio that makes the signals stronger is called the **amplifier.** Amplifiers strengthen the signal. They also "clean" it, by acting like a filter. They allow only the program sounds to come through. They cut out unwanted sounds that come from atmospheric interference.

Making waves

Try this experiment to see how waves are amplified.

1. Jiggle one end of a rope while a friend holds the other end still. You'll see a wave shape pass along the rope.

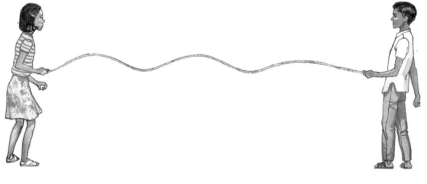

2. Now ask your friend to jiggle the rope at the same time, in time with you. The waves will get bigger.

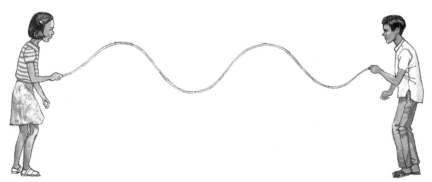

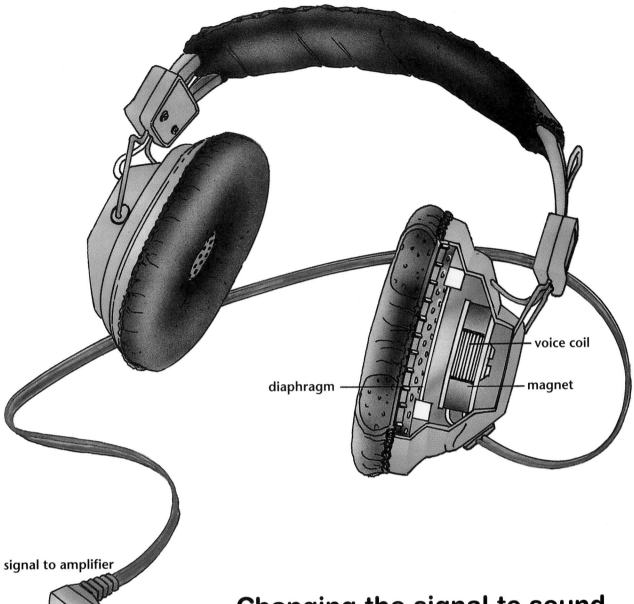

voice coil

diaphragm

magnet

signal to amplifier

Amplified sound signals are fed from the radio into the headphones. Inside the earpiece, the diaphragm vibrates and produces sound.

Changing the signal to sound

The last stage in the journey of the radio signal from the transmitter to your ears is through the speaker or headphones. There, the radio signal is converted from an electric current into a sound that you can hear.

The amplified signals enter the speaker or headphones. Inside are three main parts: a coil of wire called a **voice coil**, a cone-shaped piece of paper or plastic called a **diaphragm**, and a **magnet.** The electric waves from the amplifier pass through the voice coil and produce varying forces against the magnet's field. These forces drive the coil alternately toward and away from the magnet in rapid vibrations. In turn, the diaphragm, which is attached to the coil, also vibrates. The diaphragm's vibrations create sound waves imitating those that first went into the microphone. The ear hears these vibrations as sound.

Find out more by looking
at pages **38–39**
40–41
44–45

Inside transistors

Modern electronic equipment, such as computers and television sets, were first made possible in 1947. Why 1947? Because that was the year that the transistor was invented. A transistor is made of a tiny chip called a **semiconductor.** A semiconductor consists of layers of a special material called **silicon.** The silicon layers are treated so that they will carry, or **conduct,** electricity only in certain ways.

Transistors do two things very well. They work as simple switches or gateways, turning on or off in response to electric signals. They also are good at strengthening weak electric signals.

Your portable radio has an antenna that picks up radio waves broadcast by a distant transmitter. But these radio waves are very weak by the time they reach you. The transistors in your radio strengthen, or **amplify,** the signals. The amplified signals are fed to the radio speaker or headphones.

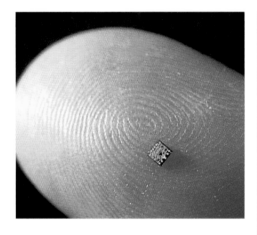

This integrated circuit, shown right, has been magnified about 200 times. The components and connections are etched on the surface of a silicon chip The chip is enclosed in plastic to protect it. The silicon chip, above, is so small that it will fit easily on your fingertip.

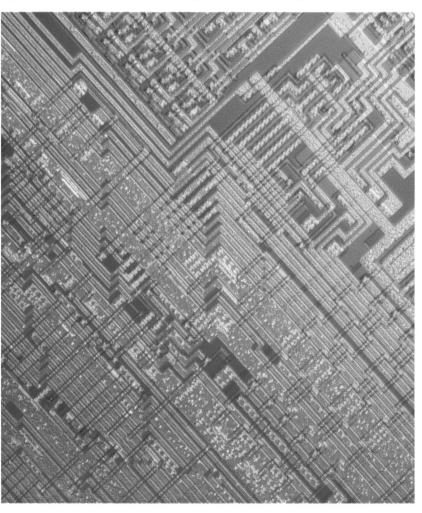

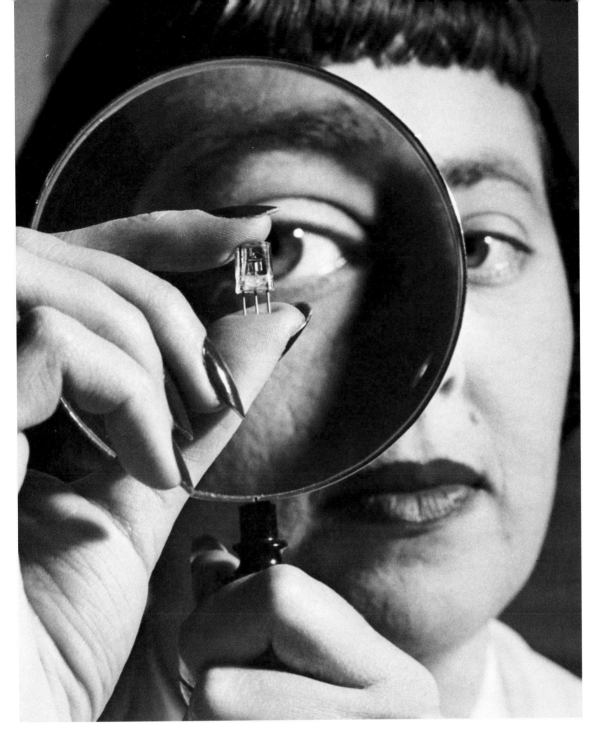

This woman is looking at an early transistor through a magnifying glass. The first transistors, used about 50 years ago, made modern equipment possible, but they were large and bulky compared to today's silicon chips.

The parts of a transistor

A transistor has three connections—the base, the collector, and the emitter. These three connections are joined to a battery or a source of direct current. A weak signal is fed into one connection, usually the **base.** Most of the energy from the power supply flows in through the **emitter** and makes the signal stronger. This amplified signal then comes out through one of the other connections—usually the **collector.**

Smaller and smaller

Transistors are one part of an electronic circuit. Electronic circuits also have several other parts that do other jobs. During the late 1950's, scientists and engineers invented a way to put all of the parts of an electronic circuit onto a single silicon chip. They replaced the wires connecting the parts with tiny metal connectors. This improvement made the new chips work faster.

These new semiconductor chips were called **integrated circuits.** Inventors soon began to develop integrated circuits for various kinds of electronic devices, from control systems for rockets to digital watches. In 1971, the first microprocessor was introduced. A microprocessor is a single integrated circuit that does all the tasks of a computer. Integrated circuit chips are found in most electronic devices and appliances. Your microwave oven, wristwatch, clock radio, cassette tape player, and television set probably all have integrated circuit chips. Today, integrated circuit chips are usually called silicon chips or, simply, chips.

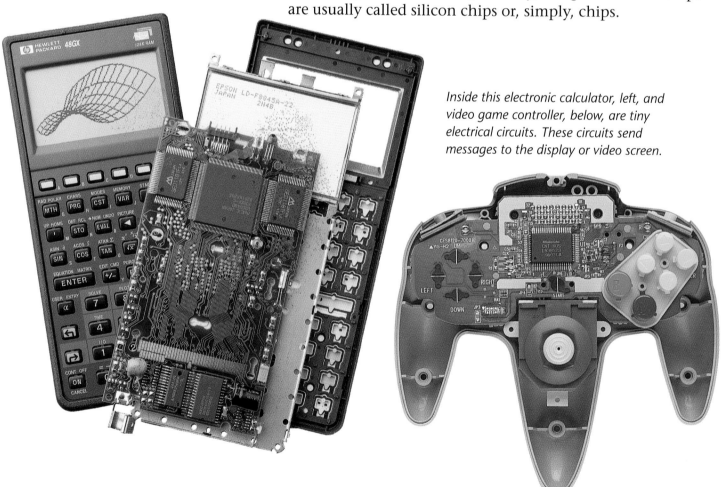

Inside this electronic calculator, left, and video game controller, below, are tiny electrical circuits. These circuits send messages to the display or video screen.

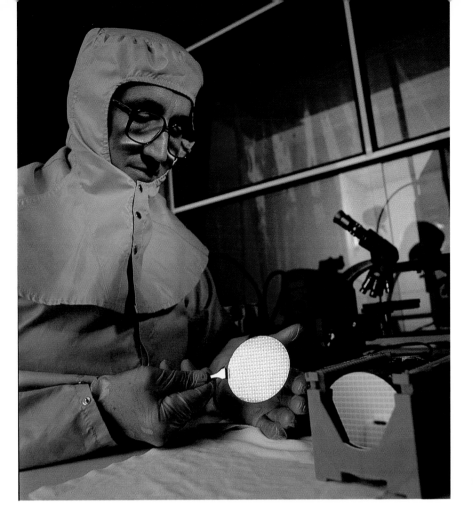

The clean room, where silicon chips are made, must be kept cleaner than a hospital operating room.

Making a silicon chip

Making a silicon chip takes many steps, and each step must be carried out perfectly or the chip will not work.

Silicon is actually a very simple, common substance—sand. The first step in making silicon crystals is to melt sand in a furnace. The melted silicon is formed into the shape of large "logs." These logs are then sliced into thin wafers of silicon.

Next, engineers may use microscopic maps of the circuits, called **masks**, to etch the correct circuit pathways onto the chips. Many chips are etched onto a single wafer. A laser cuts the chips from the wafer, and wire connections are added to each one. Finally, the chips are mounted in containers made of plastic, ceramic, or metal. The finished chips can then be installed in various kinds of electronic equipment.

Because the circuit pathways are so tiny, even a small piece of dust can ruin a chip. That's why the **clean room**, where chips are made, must be kept cleaner than an operating room in a hospital. The chips are never touched by human hands.

Find out more by looking at pages **48–49**

The television camera

Radio turns sound waves into electric signals. The signals can then be carried by radio waves from the transmitter to your home. Your radio changes them back into sound. Television works in the same way, but it turns light waves as well as sound waves into electric signals. The signals are then carried by radio waves.

The machine that picks up the light waves and starts them on their journey is called a **camera.** But it is not like a photographic camera, which takes one picture of a scene. A television camera takes thousands of tiny pictures of each scene. It can also move across the scene in an orderly pattern called **scanning.** A series of still images appears, one after the other, on your television screen. This happens so fast that the images merge, and what you see is a single, moving picture.

Sound is picked up by a microphone and changed into electric signals. The sound signal is added to the picture signal before they both go to the transmitter.

Light waves enter high-quality color cameras and are separated into the colors red, green, and blue.

These waves pass down three camera tubes or charge-coupled devices and hit three signal plates.

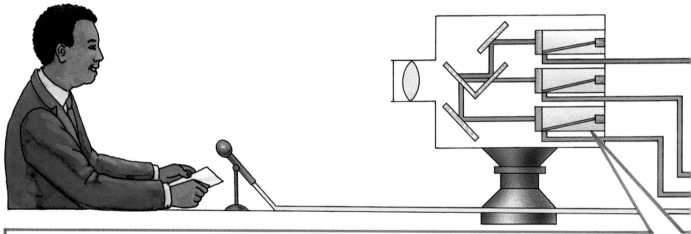

A primary color signal

is produced by a camera tube or a charge-coupled device. These produce an electric signal for each color—red, green, and blue. A total of three tubes is needed.

signal plate   camera tube   charge-coupled device

scanning lines

primary color signal

electron beam

electron gun

electric image

primary color signal

Painting with light

If you were painting this scene, you could mix each color in the picture separately. The television camera scans the colors in the picture and separates them into red, green, and blue. At the same time, the camera scans the picture for brightness and depth of color. All this information enters the camera, where it is turned into electric signals.

The control room of a television studio is where the program director chooses which pictures to send to the transmitter.

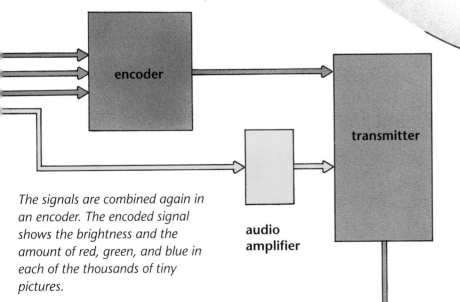

encoder

transmitter

audio amplifier

The signals are combined again in an encoder. The encoded signal shows the brightness and the amount of red, green, and blue in each of the thousands of tiny pictures.

Find out more by looking at pages **46–47**

Receiving television

Television signals can arrive at your home in three different ways. They may come along cables laid underground. They may come from a land-based transmitter that sends radio waves across Earth's surface. Or they may come from a satellite. Programs are beamed up from a transmitter to a satellite, which beams them back to Earth.

However the signals arrive, your television set has the same job to do. It receives a jumble of information in the form of electric signals. It sorts these out and turns them into pictures and sound. First, the signal is amplified by passing it through an electronic circuit. Then the sound and picture signals are separated, and then the sound signal is fed to a speaker. Finally, the picture signal is fed to the television screen.

The television tube

The television tube reverses what the television camera does. It builds up a picture by scanning light across your television screen. A television tube is shaped like a funnel. At the wide end is the screen. The back of the screen is coated with more than 300,000 dots of a chemical called **phosphor.** Phosphor glows in red, green, and blue when bursts of electricity are shot at the dots. At the narrow end of the tube are three **electron guns,** one for each color, that do the shooting.

Each electron gun receives the picture signal for one of the colors. The electron guns scan the screen with this information, just as the camera scanned the scene in front of it. This process causes a duplicate of the scene in front of the camera to appear on the TV screen.

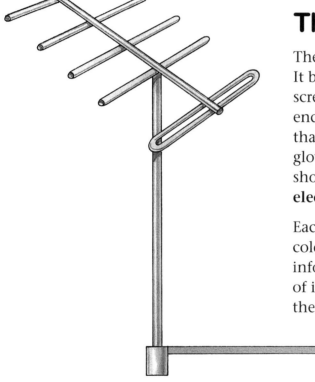

The TV antenna receives radio waves from the transmitter. The waves are turned into electric signals. A tuner selects a signal, which is then amplified and split into sound and picture signals.

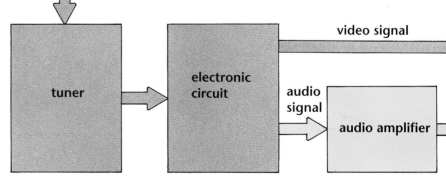

video signal

tuner

electronic circuit

audio signal

audio amplifier

Behind the TV screen is a metal shadow mask, which has rows of holes. The screen is coated with tiny phosphor dots, arranged in groups of threes. Phosphor dots glow red, green, or blue when electrons are fired at them. Three electron guns, one for each color, fire electrons through the mask.

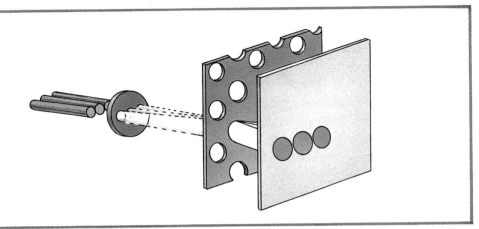

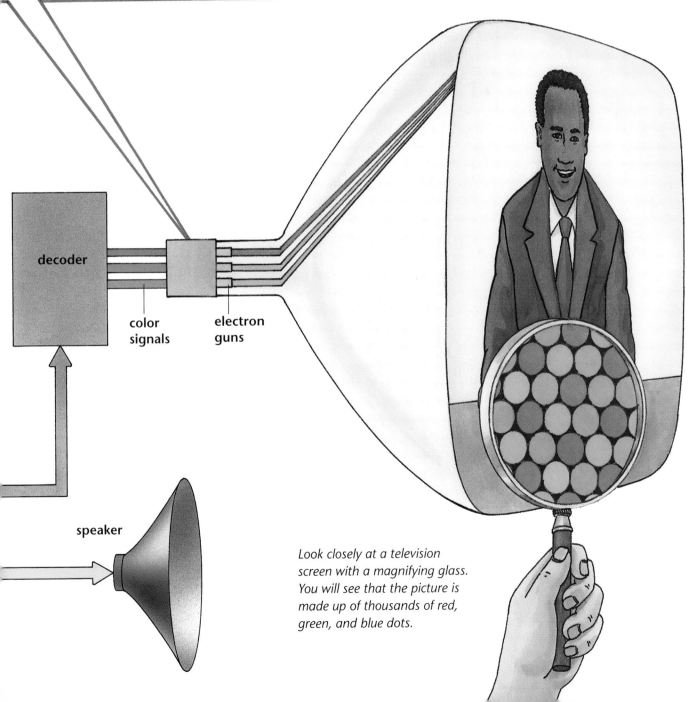

decoder

color signals

electron guns

speaker

Look closely at a television screen with a magnifying glass. You will see that the picture is made up of thousands of red, green, and blue dots.

Communications satellites

When a radio signal reaches a communications satellite, it is very weak. Before returning the signal to Earth, the satellite amplifies the signal to make it stronger.

Messages sent by communications satellites are carried on microwaves. These electromagnetic waves can travel at the speed of light—186,282 miles (299,792 kilometers) in just one second.

Solar power

Most satellites are powered by **solar batteries**, which make electricity from the light of the sun. Each satellite needs to be positioned so that rays from the sun are collected by its **solar panels.** Sometimes the satellite can make small movements to ensure that it stays facing the sun.

The Global Positioning System (GPS) is a worldwide navigation system that uses radio signals broadcast by 24 Navstar satellites. Computerized radio receivers on boats, planes, or other vehicles use the satellite signals to calculate their position. GPS can determine a user's location within 330 feet (100 meters).

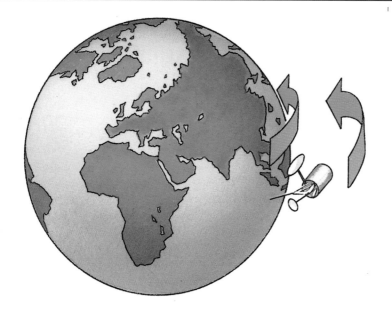

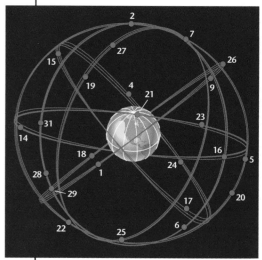

Geostationary satellites

Some satellites are **geostationary.** They seem to hover above Earth. In fact, these satellites are traveling in orbit with Earth. They remain 22,300 miles (35,900 kilometers) above a single point on Earth's surface because they travel at exactly the same speed as Earth rotates. Both satellites and planet take 24 hours to complete one rotation.

Find out more by looking at pages **26–27**

More than 20 Intelsat satellites orbit Earth, transmitting television, telephone, and other data signals. Intelsat VIII-A can handle up to 22,500 telephone calls and three color television broadcasts at the same time. Its solar panels enable it to receive energy from the sun.

The name Intelsat is short for International Telecommunications Satellite Organization.

Space trash

There are more than 2,000 satellites circling above Earth. There are also many pieces of broken satellites and space rockets. This "space trash" hurtles through space at a tremendous speed. A piece as small as a paint chip can badly damage a satellite.

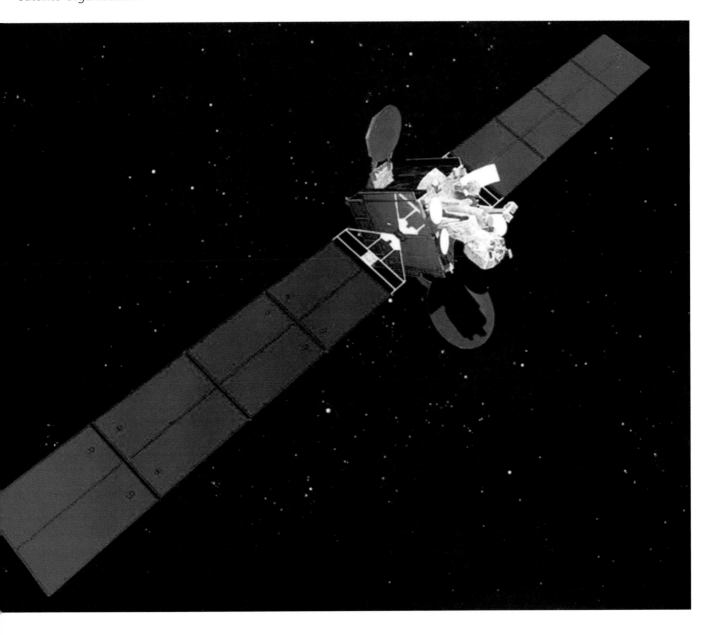

Find out more by looking at pages **26–27**

Communications on the move

There are many people who often need to make or receive telephone calls while they are away from their home or office. When they are out, someone may need to speak to them urgently.

Mobile telephones

Many busy people have a small mobile telephone that they carry with them. This mobile telephone receives calls sent by radio waves. Mobile telephones are small enough to fit in your pocket. Some mobile telephones are also called **cellular,** or **cell,** telephones because they use a special transmitter network divided into small areas called **cells.** Calls can be passed from one transmitter to another, so that someone with a mobile telephone can move from one cell into another and not lose contact with the person to whom he or she is speaking.

Beeping messages

Some people carry a small paging device, or **pager.** If someone needs to contact a person who has a pager, he or she calls a phone number assigned to the pager and dials in the number he or she wants the pager carrier to call. A computerized switching office sends a radio signal to the pager, which makes a beeping sound and displays the phone number on a small screen. The pager carrier can then go to a phone and return the call.

A pager is a device that you carry with you to let you know when you have a phone call.

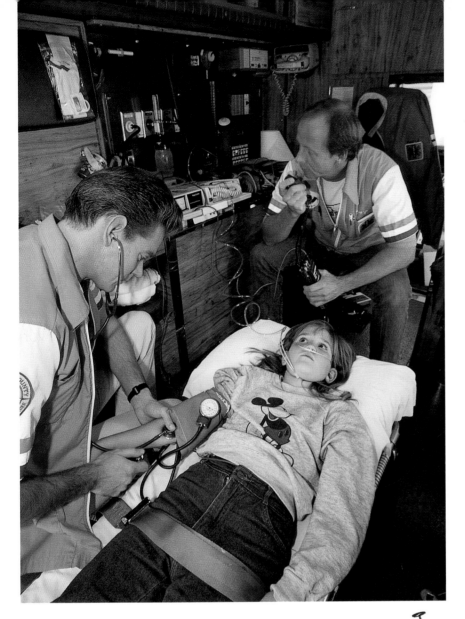

Ambulance services use two-way radios to quickly exchange messages.

Cordless phones

You can communicate while you are moving around in your own home. Many people have long extension cords on their phones or a number of phones in different rooms. But you can also buy a cordless telephone that you can carry in the house or outside with you.

Calling all cars

Police, fire, and ambulance services all use **two-way radios.** A radio transmitter links the radio to the exchange. The exchange can relay calls from one transmitter to the next. These two-way radios work on special wavelengths, so that emergency messages do not get held up by less urgent ones.

cordless phone

Leaving a message

We can speak to each other over long distances, thanks to the telephone. But how can we leave a message for someone who is not there when we call?

When you're not at home or cannot come to the phone, an **answering machine** can record messages from the people calling you. The answering machine is often a separate unit, but many telephones have built-in answering machines.

If you do not answer the phone after a certain number of rings, the caller is connected to the answering machine. The caller listens to a greeting you have recorded earlier. This greeting usually asks the caller to leave a message. The machine then records the caller's message, which can be played back later. The messages are recorded on digital chips or cassette tapes.

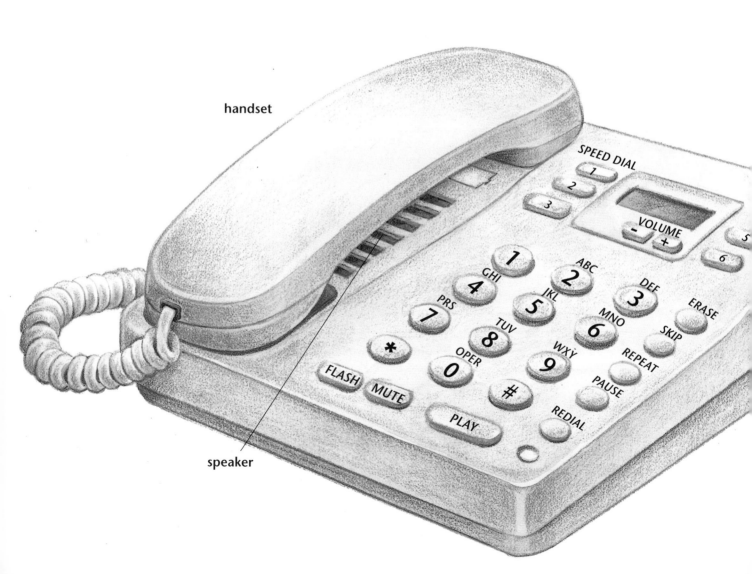

handset

speaker

Voice mail systems

Voice mail, or **voice messaging systems,** are like large, computerized answering machines. They are often used by businesses with dozens of separate phone numbers. Home voice mail services may be available through a local phone company.

The voice mail system answers the phone if you do not answer, or if you are talking on the telephone when you get another call. The caller has a choice of leaving a message or, in a business system, of being transferred to another person or to the company operator. A light on the telephone blinks to show that a message is waiting. In a home voice mail system, a special dial tone indicates that a message is waiting.

To listen to the message, you dial a special number to connect to an electronic mailbox, where your messages are stored. You can save or delete messages or forward them to other people. Some voice mail systems send a message to a pager to let a person know she or he has received a call.

Messages by light

When people first used electricity for communication, the electricity traveled along telegraph wires. Then came radio and television, which are carried on radio waves. The newest method uses glass and light.

Have you ever held a magnifying glass over a piece of paper on a sunny day? If enough of the sun's rays pass through the magnifying glass, they can burn a hole in the paper. Light is a form of energy. Some watches and calculators are powered by the energy of light.

An optical fiber is about as thick as a human hair. Optical fibers are bundled to make fiber-optic cables that can carry thousands of messages.

Laser light

In 1960, a new and powerful form of light was invented. A machine called a **laser** produces a concentrated beam of light that is many times stronger than the sun's rays passing through a magnifying glass. Because it is so strong and so concentrated, laser light can travel long distances.

Tubes of light

Like electricity, light is either on or off. So it can be used like electricity to send messages in bursts, or pulses, of energy. Laser light can travel down glass fibers, carrying messages from one place to another. The glass fibers are called **optical fibers.** They are so thin that they can be threaded through the eye of a needle! Optical fibers have replaced wires in many telephone networks.

Optical fibers are better than wires in many ways. They do not suffer from electrical interference. Laser light signals are stronger than electric signals, so fewer relays are needed. An optical fiber can carry more messages than a wire. It also resists corrosion better.

A fiber-optic cable is much lighter and smaller than metal telephone cables.

Communications today and tomorrow

New technology is changing how we communicate today and paving the way for an exciting future. On the next few pages, you'll learn about some new methods of communication.

Sound into light

Telephones convert sound waves into electric signals and send them over telephone wire. Fiber-optic communication takes those signals and turns them into pulses of laser light. The pulses of light travel through fiber-optic cables made of thin strands of glass fiber, each smaller than a human hair.

Because they use light instead of electricity, fiber-optic cables can carry more messages at faster speeds than ordinary copper wire. Fiber-optic cables are often used for long-distance telephone calls.

Videophones

Did you ever wish that you could see the person you are talking to on the telephone? A **videophone** will let you do that. Videophones transmit both a video signal, like television, and an audio signal, like a regular phone. A videophone has a small television camera and screen, along with a standard receiver and touch-tone pad.

A videophone has a TV screen and, in a round hole above the screen, a TV camera, so users can see images of each other. Ordinary lines transmit the sound and picture signals.

Television by cable

Most television stations send their signals through the air. However, cable television signals come into your home through a special kind of cable. Cable television provides a better picture and offers many more channels than regular television. Some cable television systems offer more than 100 channels. Many of these channels are devoted to special subjects, such as sports, health, comedy, movies, food, weather, or music.

To get cable television in your home, you must subscribe to the service by paying a fee. Cable systems may also be interactive—that is, you can use your cable television to shop, play games, and find information. You can even order movies and programs from a central computer and have them sent directly to your television set.

Television by satellite

Television networks send television signals from one station to another by satellite. If you have a special satellite antenna, often called a **satellite dish**, you can receive television signals directly from satellites. Most home satellite antennas are about 18 inches (45 centimeters) across. Some satellite systems offer up to 175 channels.

HDTV

The television screen you watch in the future may be one-third wider than the screen you watch now. High-definition television (HDTV) is a system being developed by several countries and television manufacturers. The picture tube on an HDTV paints the picture on your screen using more than 1,000 lines, nearly twice the number of today's televisions. The result is a picture that is much sharper and clearer than the pictures on today's televisions.

High-definition television (HDTV) produces a supersharp image, as shown on the left side of the photograph. The image on the right side was produced by a standard television set.

The innovative Internet

To connect to the Internet using a computer, you need a modem. A modem is a small device that allows two computers to exchange information over phone lines. People can also get the Internet through their television, cell phone, or pager, using special telecommunications services.

The Internet is making big changes in the way we exchange information, and these changes affect the way we live. The Internet is a huge network of computer networks, linking millions upon millions of computer users around the world. People use the Internet chiefly to send **electronic mail**, or **e-mail.** Suppose you want to send an e-mail to a friend. You type the message, fill in your friend's e-mail "address," and tell the program to send it. Almost instantly your e-mail travels through the Internet until it reaches your friend's computer.

People also use the Internet to send documents, **download,** or copy, files stored on other computers, and operate computers in distant locations. An Internet feature called the **World Wide Web** allows people to view screens called **Web sites** that include pictures, sound, and video.

People can also set up meetings with others using Internet conferencing. With this feature, you can see and hear people live over the Internet, using an Internet camera and speakers. You can also share images and data during these sessions.

Getting connected

People connect to the Internet by subscribing to an **online service.** Some services are free; others require a fee. Subscribers can look up information in electronic encyclopedias and libraries, order products, and **download** computer files. There is even a feature that allows you to "chat" with another person by typing out short messages that appear instantly on that person's computer.

Subscribers also can join Internet **newsgroups.** Newsgroups serve as places where people who share similar interests can exchange information. They "post" written messages for other people to read and respond to. Many thousands of newsgroups exist, each devoted to a special interest, such as a particular hobby, television show, or author.

Communication networks

These two students are using a modem to access articles stored by an online service.

A single, large network can connect computers with telephone companies, cable-TV stations, and other communication systems. People can bank, shop, watch TV, buy tickets, bid for items, find the best prices, and do many other things through a network. Communication networks can instantly give people a huge amount of information anywhere and anytime.

Intelligent agents are special software programs that can do a particular job over the networks. In the future, a doctor may even be able to operate on a patient in a distant city, using a system combining modems, computers, television, and robotic surgical devices. These networks are changing how we communicate, live, work, and learn.

ENERGY

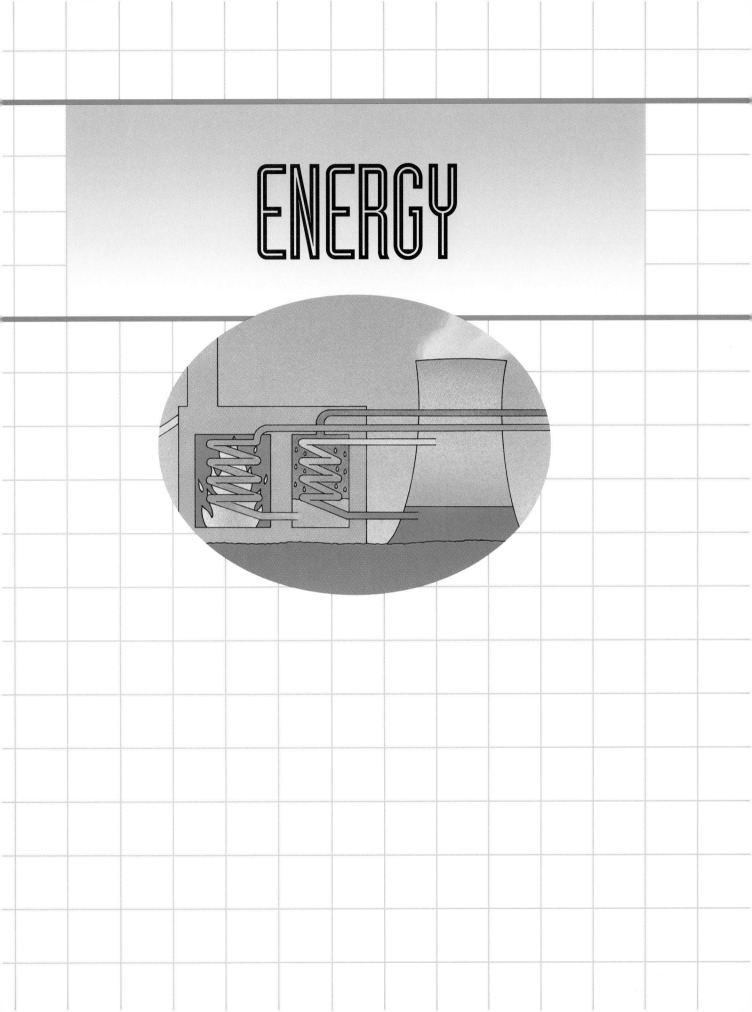

What is energy?

The world is full of movement. Trees move in the wind. Aircraft fly in the air. Ships sail on the sea. People and animals move around. None of these things can move without **energy**. Living things and machines need energy in order to work.

Where does energy come from? Almost all energy comes from the sun. The sun's energy changes into other kinds of energy when it reaches Earth. The sun's energy is even in coal and oil. Long ago, the sun gave its energy to plants and animals. When they died, their bodies turned into oil and coal over millions of years. Power stations then change the energy in coal and oil into electrical energy. Without the energy provided by the sun, there would be no life on Earth.

Food provides the energy your leg muscles need in order to ride your bicycle. The sun provides the energy needed to produce the food.

The energy that turns the blades of a windmill comes from the wind. The amount of energy produced by the windmill depends on how hard the wind blows.

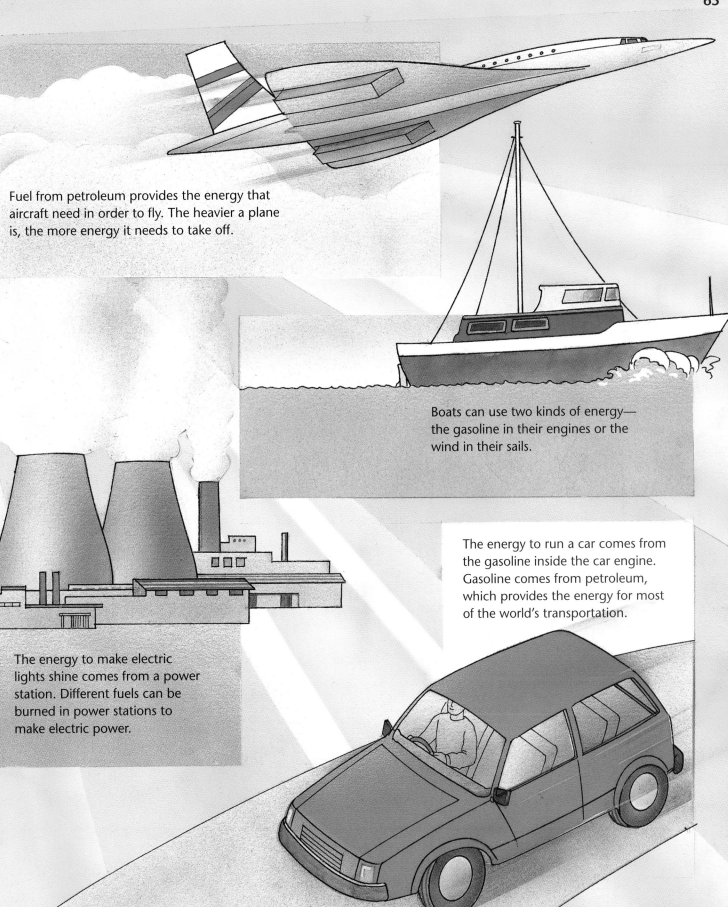

Fuel from petroleum provides the energy that aircraft need in order to fly. The heavier a plane is, the more energy it needs to take off.

Boats can use two kinds of energy—the gasoline in their engines or the wind in their sails.

The energy to run a car comes from the gasoline inside the car engine. Gasoline comes from petroleum, which provides the energy for most of the world's transportation.

The energy to make electric lights shine comes from a power station. Different fuels can be burned in power stations to make electric power.

Energy sources

How do you keep cool in your house? What kind of light do you use at night? Anything that gives you heat or light uses energy. Household appliances use energy. In your notebook, make a list of all the things in your kitchen that use energy. What kind of energy do you think each appliance uses?

In this cutaway view of a house, you can see many different energy sources. Look around your house, and make a list of all the energy sources in it.

1. solar energy collector
2. electric light
3. electric outlet
4. heat and air conditioning vent
5. gas stove
6. air conditioner
7. gas furnace
8. wood
9. wood fireplace

Energy in the home

Most homes receive a supply of electricity. The electricity travels along cables and wires from a power station. At the power station, electricity is usually made from the energy released by burning fossil fuels, or by using nuclear fuel or water power. **Fossil fuels** formed from the remains of prehistoric plants and animals. These fuels include coal, natural gas, and petroleum, from which we get oil.

Besides electricity, fossil fuels are also used as a source of energy in our homes. Wood, coal, and oil can be burned to give heat. Natural gas can be burned for heating and cooking. Oil lamps and gasoline lanterns can be used as a source of light.

Other sources of energy in the home include solar energy and wind power. **Solar energy** is energy from the sun, often gathered by solar panels. Solar energy can warm a house or heat up water. Wind power is often impractical unless there are strong, steady winds.

Using up energy sources

Fossil fuels are called **nonrenewable sources** of energy because, once they have been used up, they cannot be replaced. One day, all the coal, natural gas, and oil on Earth may be used up. There will then be no more available.

Sources of energy that can be used over and over again are called **renewable,** or **inexhaustible,** sources. Solar energy, wind power, and water power are renewable energy sources. No matter how much we use them, there will always be plenty more.

Find out more by looking at pages **114–115**

Wood, coal, gas, and charcoal can all be fuels for cooking. These people in Kenya are cooking their food over a charcoal fire.

The iron and other materials in this furnace have become so hot that they have melted into a liquid. The liquid steel is then poured out of the furnace and left to cool and harden.

Atoms and molecules

Do you know what you are made of? One answer is that you are made of flesh, blood, and bone. Another answer is that you are made of atoms and molecules. **Atoms** are tiny bits of matter that join to make everything in the world. An atom is more than a million times smaller than the thickness of a human hair. Atoms come together to form groups called **molecules.** Powerful microscopes produce pictures of atoms and molecules. We cannot see them directly.

What is kinetic energy?

Atoms and molecules are in motion all the time. They have **kinetic energy.** The word *kinetic* comes from a Greek word meaning "to move."

In a solid object like a bar of iron, the atoms are packed close together. When the iron bar is cold, they vibrate only a little. When the iron bar is heated up, the atoms start to move faster and faster. The quicker the atoms move, the more kinetic energy they have. If the iron bar becomes hot enough, the atoms have so much kinetic energy that they can separate from each other. Then the solid iron melts and becomes a liquid.

Making steam

When a liquid is heated, some of its molecules may gain enough energy to escape from the surface of the liquid and into the air. The escaped molecules change their form and become a gas. This is what happens when you boil a kettle of water. Some of the molecules in the water escape and make an invisible gas called **steam.** As steam contacts cool air, the steam **condenses** turning into tiny drops of liquid water. It is a cloud of these drops that we see.

If you have ever seen a steam train or a steamship, you will have noticed condensed steam pouring out of a funnel on top. Inside these trains and ships, there are steam engines. These engines use steam to make the train or ship move. The largest and fastest ships have powerful steam engines, called turbines.

Steam drives the engine that makes this train move along. The steam is made by a boiler next to the firebox, which produces the smoke seen in the picture.

From ice to water

You will need:

two ice cubes

two saucers

a timer

1. Put one ice cube on a saucer. While the ice remains frozen, the molecules inside the ice vibrate only slowly. Time how long it takes for the ice cube to melt completely.

2. Put the second ice cube on the second saucer. Start the timer. Place one finger on the ice cube and hold it there until the ice cube melts completely. (Switch to another finger if the first one gets too cold.) The warmth from your finger makes the molecules vibrate more quickly. The kinetic energy of the molecules makes the ice turn to water. Time how long it takes for the ice cube to melt completely.

Did one ice cube melt more quickly than the other? If so, do you know why?

This fireworks display uses a lot of chemical energy. The colors in the fireworks are produced from the burning of different chemicals.

Energy locked up in chemicals

Have you ever been to a display of **chemical energy**? You probably have, but you called it something else. At a display of chemical energy, there are usually many different colored lights and a lot of noise. Rockets shoot up into the sky. Firecrackers make loud bangs. Pinwheels spin around very quickly. Stars shoot out of Roman candles.

Yes, fireworks use chemical energy. Fireworks are made of a special exploding powder called **gunpowder,** as well as other explosive chemicals. These chemicals contain lots of energy. When gunpowder burns, it releases large amounts of different gases. These gases are released at great speed. So the energy escapes quickly and with lots of noise into the air. The colored lights of the fireworks are made by burning other chemicals.

Find out more by looking at pages **68–69**

When a firework has finished burning, all that is left inside is some black powder that does not burn. The high-energy chemicals in the gunpowder have been changed into high-energy, moving gases. These gases have created kinetic energy of motion and sound. The change that takes place inside the firework is called a **chemical change.**

Chemical change

Fireworks are just one example of a chemical change. There are many more examples taking place all around you. Car engines use chemical energy, too. High-energy molecules of gasoline are burned inside most car engines. The gasoline molecules turn into gas molecules that produce kinetic energy.

Chemical energy can also be produced without burning. Animals and humans use chemical energy in food. They use the chemical energy to work and keep warm. Light energy from the sun can also be changed into chemical energy. This happens when sunlight reaches the leaves of plants. The plants trap this energy and use it to make a special substance called **glucose.** The glucose contains chemical energy. Living things can get energy from glucose.

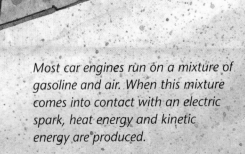

Most car engines run on a mixture of gasoline and air. When this mixture comes into contact with an electric spark, heat energy and kinetic energy are produced.

Nuclear energy

Chemical energy is one kind of energy that is "locked up" inside atoms and molecules. Another kind is **nuclear energy.**

In the center of every atom is the **nucleus.** This is made of tiny particles called **protons** and **neutrons.** Protons have a positive electric charge. Neutrons have no electric charge. The nucleus is surrounded by **electrons,** which have a negative charge. The positively charged protons and negatively charged electrons attract each other. Each atom is held together by this force of attraction.

Splitting atoms

Most atoms can be arranged into different groups to make different substances. The atoms of a few metals can be changed, or split, to make new, different atoms. The nucleus of an atom of a metal called uranium can be split into two. This is called **nuclear fission.** The word "fission" means "breaking apart."

When the nucleus of a uranium atom is split, some of its neutrons escape. These neutrons crash into other uranium atoms, causing them to split. As the nucleus of the atom is split, it releases huge amounts of heat. In a nuclear power station, this heat energy is used to produce electricity.

Fusing atoms

The nuclei of the atoms of the gas hydrogen cannot be split, but they can be squeezed together. This process is called **nuclear fusion.** The word "fusion" means "joining."

The sun's energy comes from the nuclear fusion of hydrogen atoms. The hydrogen atoms in the sun continually crash into each other and fuse, making larger atoms of helium gas.

A type of hydrogen gas called deuterium is heated to extremely high temperatures. The deuterium atoms crash into each other and form heavier elements. This process releases large amounts of energy. Scientists are trying to find a way of using nuclear fusion in power stations because it will be one of the cheapest and cleanest ways of producing electricity.

73

Find out more by looking at pages **68–69**
102–103

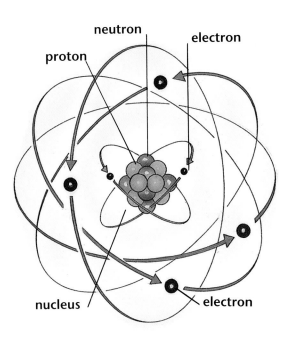

An atom is made up of three different types of particles—protons, neutrons, and electrons. The protons and neutrons are crowded into the nucleus near the center of the atom. The electrons go around the nucleus at fantastic speeds.

The photograph on the left shows the mushroom-shaped cloud that rises up into the air following a nuclear explosion.

Find out more by looking
at pages **86–87**
90–91

Energy from food

You use energy all the time, even when you're asleep. You need energy for your body to work. You need energy to keep warm. When the weather is cold, or when you take part in sports, you need extra amounts of energy to help your body and muscles work harder.

Your energy comes from the food you eat. Food contains chemical energy. As the food is broken down, your body uses the energy to keep warm and to do work. Do you know which foods contain large amounts of chemical energy?

Breaking down the food

Scientists have been able to figure out the amounts of chemical energy in different foods. The amount of energy in food is measured in units called **calories.** A plateful of lettuce, for example, has few calories and therefore very little energy. Rice and bananas contain much more energy. But an equal amount of ice cream contains even more!

When you eat food, it travels through your body to your stomach and intestines. Special chemicals called **enzymes** in your stomach help break down the food into different substances that your body can use. We call this breaking-down process **digestion.** The substances from food that produce energy for your body most efficiently are called **fats** and **carbohydrates.** Fats, such as butter and oil, and carbohydrates, such as bread, potatoes, and sugars, are high in calories.

You can see from this chart how much energy you'll get from eating 7 ounces (200 grams) of each of these different foods. The tomatoes have about 40 calories. The ice cream has about 400!

ice cream

rice

eggs

bananas

tomatoes

Your body needs energy

Different people need different amounts of energy from their food. A person doing heavy work, like digging or sawing wood, or an Arctic explorer in the freezing cold needs a lot more energy than an office worker. Active children need about the same amount of energy as adults doing light work. Older people usually do less work and move around more slowly, so they need less energy.

It is important to eat only as much food as your body needs to keep your weight and energy at a comfortable level. It is also important to eat the right kinds of foods. Besides fats and carbohydrates, your body also needs proteins such as fish, meat, and cheese. **Protein** is necessary for the growth and maintenance of body structures.

These hurdlers are using up a lot of energy. They need to eat the kinds of food that contain large amounts of energy, like pasta, breads, and cereals.

The amount of food energy you need depends on your age and the activity or work you do.

men

young people

women

schoolgirl

infant 1–3 years

Find out more by looking
at pages **68–69**
90–91

Potential energy

"On your marks! Get set! Go!" These are the orders the starter shouts when you take part in a running race. When you are running, your body has a lot of kinetic energy, the energy of movement. When you are "on your marks," you use a small amount of energy. Most of your energy is stored, or saved up, ready for the running of the race. Energy that is stored for later use is called **potential energy.**

Potential energy is often linked to work that has already been done. Take a ball and place it on the floor. Now put the ball on a high shelf. The ball has more potential energy when it is on the shelf than it has on the floor. The ball has gained this extra energy because work was done when the ball was placed on the high shelf. Do you know how to turn the potential, or stored, energy of the ball into kinetic, or moving, energy?

These in-line skaters are using a lot of kinetic energy.

How is energy stored?

An archer's bow has potential energy when it is bent. When the archer releases the bow's string, this potential energy changes into kinetic energy, and the arrow shoots forward. When you wind up a clock, potential energy is stored in the clock's spring. This energy changes into the kinetic energy that makes the clock work.

The potential energy of this archer's bent bow will turn into kinetic energy when the archer releases the bow's string.

Make a spool tractor

Find out how a spool tractor uses a twisted rubber band to store potential energy.

You will need:

a 1/2-inch (1.25-centimeter) circular slice of a candle with a hole in the center (to slice the candle, use a dinner knife that has been held under very hot water)

a rubber band

two toothpicks

an empty thread spool

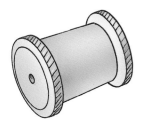

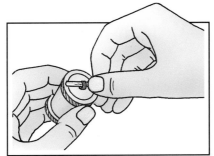

1. Push the rubber band through the center of the spool. Break one of the toothpicks in half and push one half through the loop of the band at one end of the spool.

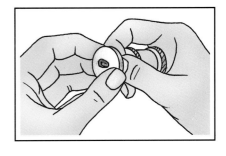

2. Push the other end of the rubber band through the hole in the candle.

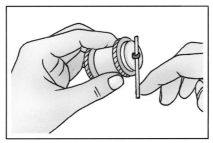

3. Push the second toothpick through the loop of the rubber band at the candle end. Wind up the tractor very tightly by turning this toothpick.

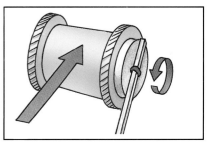

4. Place the tractor on the floor. Describe what happens using the terms "potential energy" and "kinetic energy."

Sound energy

Have you ever heard a jet airplane when it is getting ready to take off? The noise that the plane makes is sometimes so loud that you cannot hear anything else.

Sounds moving through the air

Sound is a type of energy. Sounds are produced when an object vibrates. When this happens, the air around the object also vibrates. These vibrations in the air travel as **sound waves.** A jet engine makes a great deal of sound energy. The engine sounds loud when it is close, but you can sometimes hear the noise even when the plane is several miles away from you.

A "look" at sound

Here is an experiment that you can do to demonstrate that sound energy moves through the air.

You will need:

a piece of clear plastic wrap

a rubber band

a spoon

some rice grains

an empty glass jar

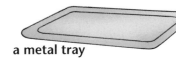
a metal tray

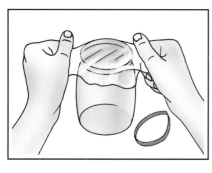

1. Stretch the plastic tightly over the open end of the jar. Use the rubber band to keep the plastic in position.

2. Sprinkle a few rice grains over the plastic.

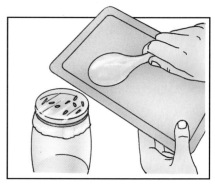

3. Hold the metal tray close to the jar and bang it with the spoon. What happens? Write down your observations in your notebook. Explain what you saw.

People who work on airport runways need to protect their ears from the noise of the aircraft engines. They wear protective gear over their ears.

Rippling vibrations

Think of the ripples on a small lake when you throw a pebble into the calm water. If the lake is big enough, the ripples become smaller and smaller until they disappear altogether before they reach the edge of the lake. In the same way, sound spreads out in waves from the place where it is first made. The sound waves, like the ripples in the lake, become weaker the farther they travel. The energy of the waves becomes more spread out.

Scientists use units called **decibels** to measure the intensity of sound. The sound of whispering measures about 20 decibels. The noise from a jumbo jet taking off at close range measures about 140 decibels. If sound measures more than 140 decibels, it is dangerous and can seriously damage your hearing.

The sound of a purring cat is soft and gentle, but the noise made by a jumbo jet is loud and harsh.

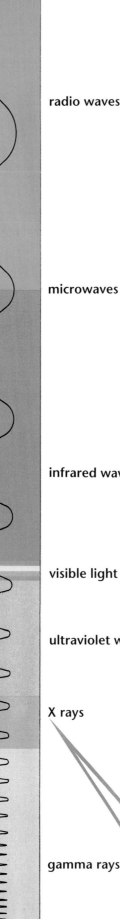

radio waves

microwaves

infrared waves

visible light

ultraviolet waves

X rays

gamma rays

Electromagnetic energy

What do you think the air is made of? It is made of millions of tiny, fast-moving particles. Waves of energy pass through the air, too. This kind of energy, called **electromagnetic energy**, is made of vibrations of electricity and magnetism. There is a whole range of different electromagnetic waves.

Some electromagnetic waves vibrate very fast. These waves have a great deal of energy. Other waves vibrate slowly and have less energy. Some of the most energetic electromagnetic waves are called X rays. X rays are used in hospital machines to photograph the inside of a person's body. When an X-ray photograph is taken, your body receives a very short burst of X-ray energy.

These colored bands represent the whole range of electromagnetic waves. Gamma rays have the most energy. Radio waves have the least energy.

X rays can show if a patient has any broken bones. If someone has swallowed something metal, that will show up, too.

The speed of electromagnetic waves

There are many different types of electromagnetic waves, but in one way they are all similar. They travel through space at the same speed as light—186,282 miles (299,792 kilometers) per second. Electromagnetic waves can travel around the world more than seven times in one second. When you watch a sports telecast that is a live transmission from 3,100 miles (5,000 kilometers) away, you are seeing the picture at almost exactly the same moment as the athletes are actually competing.

It takes about eight minutes for light waves from the sun to reach us on Earth. Other stars are even farther away. It takes light waves about four years to travel from the closest stars to Earth. Scientists say that these stars are **light-years** away from Earth.

Light and heat energy travel through the air as different kinds of electromagnetic waves. Sunlight travels to Earth as light waves. The heat from the sun travels as infrared waves. Radio waves bring us radio and television.

stars

light waves

sun

light waves

Earth

An electromagnetic wave can circle Earth more than seven times in one second. Light waves reach Earth from the sun in about eight minutes. Light waves from other stars take years to reach us.

Find out more by looking at pages **76–77**

The energy in this roller coaster at a fairground changes from potential energy to kinetic energy as the car goes down the track.

Changing energy

Do you remember the ball that was full of potential, or stored, energy while resting on the shelf? If you push the ball off the shelf, its potential energy will change into kinetic energy.

Every form of energy can change into another form of energy. Coal is a fuel that contains stored chemical energy. When coal burns, the chemical energy inside it changes into heat energy.

Energy in a swinging pendulum

Follow energy as a pendulum swings.

1. Make the modeling clay into a ball. This is the weight of the pendulum. Tie one end of the string around the weight.

2. Tie the other end of the string to a hook, or something else, so that the weight can swing freely.

3. Give the weight a push to start it swinging. Can you locate the point at which the pendulum exhibits only potential energy? The point at which it exhibits only kinetic energy?

You will need:

a piece of string, 2 feet (60 centimeters) long

modeling clay

When the weight is swinging at its lowest point, it has kinetic energy but no potential energy. When the weight reaches the highest point of its swing, it stops for an instant. It has potential energy but no kinetic energy.

Can we create or destroy energy?

Energy may change in form, but it can't be made out of nothing, and neither can it be destroyed. A power station does not create the electric energy we use in our homes. The power station changes the chemical energy of the fuel into electric energy. When we use electricity, we don't destroy the electric energy. Instead, we change this energy into another form of energy, such as heat or light.

Energy on the move

How can energy move, or be **transferred**, from one object to another?

1. Tie the long piece of string between the backs of two chairs. Make sure the string is stretched fairly taut, as shown.

2. Make two weights from the modeling clay, and tie one of the short pieces of string around each weight.

3. Tie the weights onto the long piece of string.

4. Start one weight swinging gently. What happens to the second weight?

Soon the second weight will stop swinging. Why do you think this happens? After a while, the second weight will start to swing again. Think of an explanation. Write down your observations in your notebook.

You will need:

two chairs

three pieces of string, one about 30 inches (75 centimeters) long and two about 16 inches (40 centimeters) long

modeling clay

Energy converters

Imagine you are on a camping trip. You feel tired at the end of the day and want a hot meal. You've taken with you some soup and matches. You've also brought an aluminum saucepan. Woods nearby supply you with dry twigs.

When you make a campfire, heat the saucepan, and eat your soup, a scientific process takes place. By setting fire to the wood, you change, or **convert**, the stored chemical energy in the twigs into heat energy. This heat energy warms the soup. After you have eaten the soup, your body turns the chemical energy in the soup into potential energy. Your body will turn it into kinetic energy for use on the camping trip.

Your body is an **energy converter.** Some of the chemical energy you take in as food is converted into potential energy and then into kinetic energy. Some of the chemical energy is converted into heat energy to maintain body temperature.

Converting energy

We need to change one kind of energy into another in our homes. A toaster changes electric energy into heat energy. An electric light bulb converts electric energy into heat and light energy. If you look around your house, you'll soon realize there are a number of energy converters at home.

This family is using the heat energy from their campfire to cook their food. The food they eat contains chemical energy that their bodies will convert into kinetic energy or into potential energy—stored energy that their bodies can use later.

85

Find out more by looking
at pages 74–75
104–105
108–109

*The solar panels on top of this
house convert the sun's energy
to electric power.*

Old and new energy converters

For thousands of years, people have made many different
kinds of energy converters. One of the earliest kinds was the
waterwheel. Moving water pushed the blades attached to
the wheel, and this made the wheel turn. Waterwheels were
often joined to large millstones. As the waterwheel turned, it
turned the millstones, which then ground corn or wheat.
The waterwheel converted the potential energy of the falling
water into kinetic energy for grinding the grain.

A **solar cell** is a modern kind of energy converter. It converts
light energy from the sun into electric energy. Solar cells can
be used to make calculators, radios, and telephones work.
Solar cells are also used to operate telecommunications
satellites that orbit Earth.

Work and energy

Do you know that you are working when you are playing? To a scientist, work is any kind of action that uses energy.

Energy is needed to do all types of work, because something does not move unless you push or pull it. And it doesn't stop moving unless something else slows it down. When you catch a ball, for example, your hand can feel the ball pushing as it tries to continue moving. **Inertia** is the principle that says an object at rest continues to stay at rest, and an object in motion continues to move.

Pushes and pulls that change an object's motion are called **forces.** Forces are needed to overcome inertia. Forces are produced by applying energy. The more force applied, the more energy used and the more work done.

Energy for lifting

When you lift a heavy box, potential energy changes to kinetic energy in your muscles. For example, you use more energy and do more work when you move a heavy box than when you lift a lighter box for the same distance. If you carry a pile of books weighing 22 pounds (10 kilograms) up a flight of stairs, you do twice as much work as if you carried an 11-pound (5-kilogram) pile up the same flight of stairs. Since work is equal to force times distance, the energy you use is equal to the weight of the books times the distance you moved.

Inertia at work

You can do a simple experiment to learn about inertia.

You will need:

a small model car

a sheet of paper

1. Place the sheet of paper on a polished table so that the edge of the paper just sticks out over the table edge.

2. Place the model car in the middle of the paper.

3. With a quick, forceful movement, pull the paper toward you. What happens?

You may have to try this experiment several times before you obtain perfect results.

This Iraqi woman is using a great deal of energy to carry the pile of bricks on her head.

Find out more by looking at pages **68–69**

Conducted heat

Have you ever taken a spoon out of a mug of hot cocoa or some other hot drink? Did you find that the spoon was too hot to hold, so that you had to drop it? If you have never done this, don't try it now. But if you have done this, then you found out the hard way that heat can travel through some solid materials, such as metals. When heat travels in this way, we say that the heat is **conducted**.

Why was the handle of the spoon so hot? In the hot drink, the heat is conducted from the liquid into the metal spoon. Atoms in the bowl of the spoon move faster and bump harder into one another as they heat up. The faster the atoms vibrate, the hotter the spoon becomes. The atoms in the lower part of the spoon then bump into the metal atoms a littler farther up the spoon. These atoms then bump against their neighbors even farther up and make them vibrate faster. Soon, all the atoms in the spoon are vibrating faster.

Ouch! This metal spoon has heated up in the hot drink. The atoms in the metal have conducted the heat up to the spoon's handle, and it is now too hot to hold.

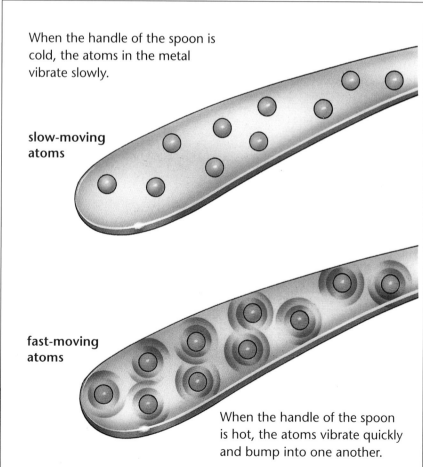

When the handle of the spoon is cold, the atoms in the metal vibrate slowly.

slow-moving atoms

fast-moving atoms

When the handle of the spoon is hot, the atoms vibrate quickly and bump into one another.

What are conductors and insulators?

A material that allows heat to travel through it, like the metal spoon, is called a **conductor.** Some materials are better conductors of heat than others. Such metals as iron, steel, and copper are good conductors. They also allow electricity to flow easily through them. Other materials, such as rubber, wood, glass, and some plastics, are poor conductors. A material that does not conduct heat or electricity easily is called an **insulator.**

Firefighters wear heat-reflective suits to protect them from flames and heat. These suits are made of a flame-resistant material and coated with aluminum or another metal to reflect heat.

Protection from heat and cold

Insulators are useful materials. The handle of a saucepan, for example, is often made of plastic or wood. This stops the conduction of heat from the pan to the handle. Firefighters wear clothes made from another good insulating material called **fiberglass.** The fiberglass prevents the heat of a fire from reaching the firefighter's body.

Air is a good insulator, too. This is why we wear wool clothes to keep warm in cold weather. Wool traps plenty of air between its fibers. Special insulated underwear provides air spaces that help retain body heat. Can you think of any other ways in which we use insulators to keep away heat, or keep it in?

Find out more by looking
at pages **68–69**
76–77
84–85

Storing energy

Before the first signs of cold weather appear in some parts of the world, animals such as squirrels and dormice have already been building up their stores of acorns, nuts, berries, and other food. Such behavior is triggered by chemical changes in the animals' bodies. They are preparing themselves for the cold months ahead, during which food will be in short supply.

The food stores of these animals contain chemical energy. As they eat the stored food, the energy is converted to body fat that will help provide them with energy during the cold weather. In the same way, a pile of firewood or a tank full of oil is a store of energy that can be burned to help keep our houses warm during the cold times of the year. This kind of stored energy is called **chemical energy.**

Stored food provides squirrels with food during the cold months.

Springs and wheels

When a clock or watch is wound up, energy is transferred from you and stored inside it. The spring inside the clock becomes a store of potential energy as it is coiled. Later, as the spring unwinds, the potential energy is released as kinetic energy to turn the hands of the clock.

Some steam engines use a heavy wheel called a **flywheel** to store energy. Steam pushes a device called a **piston** backward and forward. This produces short, sharp bursts of energy. The flywheel stores this energy and rotates smoothly. In a moving steam train, energy is stored in the rotating driving wheels. Energy is also stored in the actual weight of the moving train. Although the pistons produce bursts of energy, the heavy train can still move smoothly along the track.

Steam trains carry a supply of coal or wood as their energy store. When the coal or wood is burned, it produces kinetic energy that is stored in the train's driving wheels.

Storing electricity

Electric energy can be stored in special batteries that can be recharged. These are often called **storage batteries**, because energy is stored, or collected, inside them.

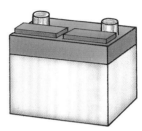

Cars have **rechargeable batteries**. When a car is moving, some of the kinetic energy produced by its engine is converted into electric energy, which is stored in the battery as chemical energy. This stored energy is needed to start the car next time. It can also be used to make the car lights work even when the engine is switched off.

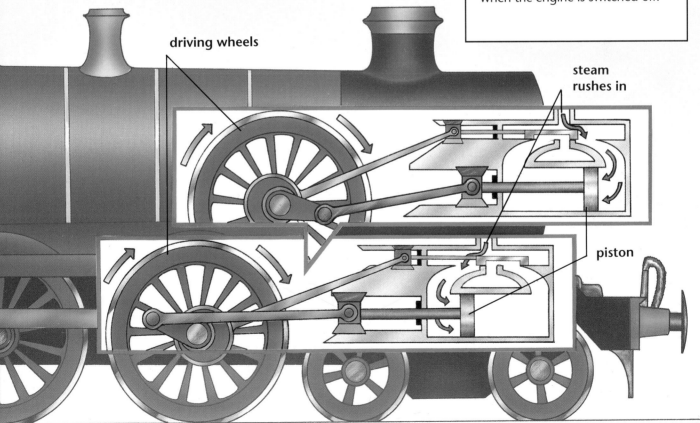

driving wheels

steam rushes in

piston

Supplying energy

Humans need energy every day and night of the year in order to survive. Factories use energy to make their machines work. We need energy in our homes for cooling, heating, lighting, and cooking. Energy is needed to light up city streets at night. All types of transportation rely on energy in one form or another.

We can obtain this energy from two sources. We can use nonrenewable energy sources, such as oil and coal, and convert the chemical energy from these sources into kinetic or electric energy. Or we can use renewable energy sources such as the sun, the wind, and flowing water.

A problem with some types of energy is that the energy is not always in the right place at the right time, and sometimes it is not there in sufficient quantity. On a cold, dark day, we turn on the heat to keep us warm and turn on lights to help us see. On such days, power stations fueled by nonrenewable energy sources usually supply as much electricity as we need.

But the same may not be true of renewable energy sources. Solar power works best when the sun is shining. On a cold, dark day, there may not be enough energy stored in solar cells to give us sufficient warmth and light. In a storm, there may be more wind energy than we can use. But when the weather is calm, there may not be enough wind to produce any energy.

These wind turbines near Altamont Pass in California deliver electricity to nearly 1 million people.

How can we store energy?

Stores of energy are important. They allow us to save energy when it is plentiful so that we can use it when it is scarce. For instance, many campers and boat owners use **generators** to make their own electricity. These generators are powered by the wind to make electricity. Rechargeable batteries are connected to the generators so that when the wind blows strongly, electricity is stored and then used on calm days.

Wires and pipelines

Energy often needs to be moved from the place where it is produced or stored to the place where it is required. For instance, wires carry electricity from power stations to homes and factories. Pipelines carry oil and natural gas from the platforms that take them out of the ground. The pipelines may stretch for thousands of miles, either underground or above the ground, to places where the fuel is made ready for homes, factories, offices, and farms.

Find out more by looking at pages **66–67**
98–99
108–109

A pipeline carries oil across Alaska. Oil is also transported by huge tankers.

The sun is a powerhouse

Did you know that the sun is really a star? It looks much larger than the stars we see in the sky at night. Although many of those stars are even larger than the sun, they look smaller because they are so far away from Earth.

All stars produce huge amounts of energy. Each star is like a powerhouse of energy. In one second, for example, the sun converts 4 million short tons (3.6 million metric tons) of matter to energy. Without the sun's energy, Earth would be completely dark and freezing cold.

Heat energy travels from the core of the sun to its surface. Energy is released from the sun's surface as electromagnetic radiation.

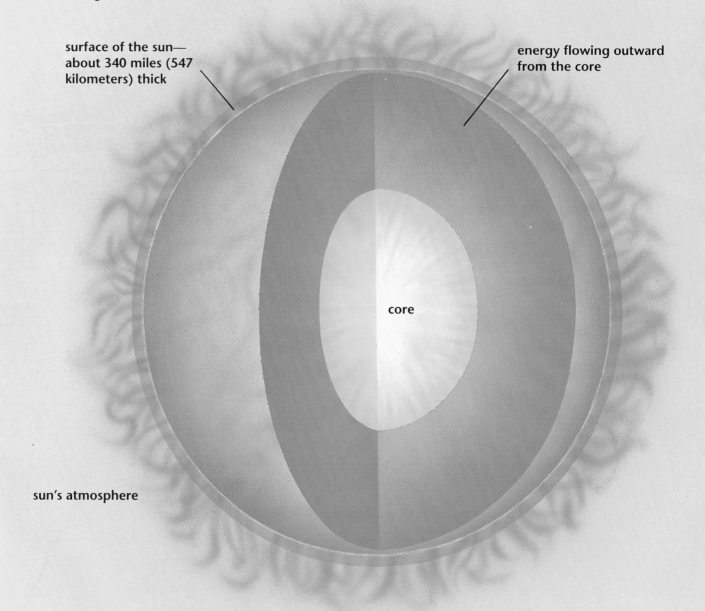

surface of the sun—about 340 miles (547 kilometers) thick

energy flowing outward from the core

core

sun's atmosphere

Find out more by looking at pages **72–73**
80–81

What is the sun?

The sun is a huge ball of hot substances. The hottest part is in the center, or **core**. Here, the fierce heat causes atoms of hydrogen to join in the process called **nuclear fusion**. During nuclear fusion, huge amounts of energy are released. This energy flows outward from the core to the surface of the sun.

The surface of the sun is like a sea of tremendously hot gases. Much of the sun's energy is heat and light that travels out, or **radiates**, in all directions. The sun is the source of almost all the energy we use.

A fountain of gas flares up from the surface of the sun, reaching as far as 1,000,000 miles (1,600,000 kilometers) into space.

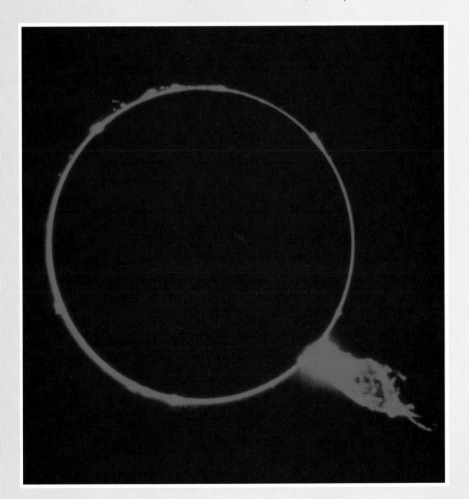

Will the sun burn itself out?

If the sun is producing so much heat and light, why doesn't it burn itself out like a coal fire or a match? The answer is that it will burn itself out, one day. It will swell up into a giant red star and use up the rest of its fuel. But don't worry—that day is about 5 billion years away!

Fossil fuels

How old is a lump of coal? This sounds like a trick question, but it isn't. Coal is millions of years old. **Anthracite**, the oldest and hardest coal, is about 400 million years old. All those years ago, many parts of Earth were covered with wet, marshlike areas of land, called swamps. Huge trees, giant ferns, mosses, and other plants grew in these swamps. As the trees and plants lost their leaves or died, the leaves and dead material formed into layers of rotting vegetation. In time, pressure from above packed these layers together to form a layer of soft material called **peat**. Peat is found throughout the world in swamps and marshes. It can be cut, dried and burned as fuel.

Sometimes, mud and sand were washed over the layers of rotting vegetation, pressing them even tighter together. This made a soft, brown kind of coal called **lignite**. As more mud and sand piled on top, the vegetation was pressed down even deeper. Movement inside Earth's crust helped to turn the lignite into hard, black **coal**. Sometimes, if you look closely at a piece of coal, you can see the outlines of a leaf from a fern that was alive millions of years ago.

Oil and gas

The formation of oil was similar to the formation of coal. Millions of years ago, small plants and animals that lived in the seas sank down to the seabed when they died. They were crushed under layers of mud and gradually turned into oil. As oil formed, it gave off natural gas. The oil and gas seeped upward until they reached layers of hard rock and became trapped under the rock.

Peat is dug out of the ground and dried. It can then be burned as fuel.

Energy from the sun

Coal, oil, and natural gas are called **fossil fuels.** They were formed from the remains of plants and animals that died long ago. When these plants and animals were alive, they converted energy from the sun into chemical energy. When we burn fossil fuels, we turn this chemical energy back into heat energy and light energy. In other words, we are releasing from these fuels the energy that first came to Earth from the sun millions of years ago.

These fossil ferns show the kinds of plants that decayed and eventually turned into coal millions of years ago.

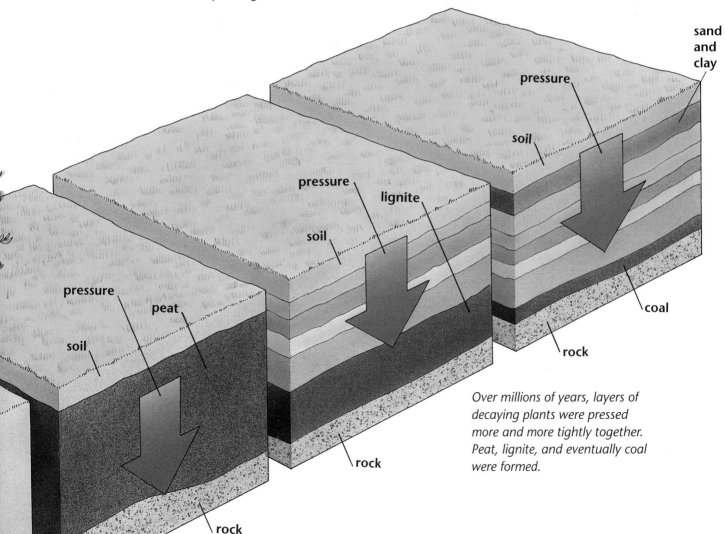

Over millions of years, layers of decaying plants were pressed more and more tightly together. Peat, lignite, and eventually coal were formed.

Making electricity

Why is electricity the most convenient form of energy to use? It is clean. It can travel over long distances along wires. It can easily be changed into other forms of energy, such as heat and light. To use the electricity connected to your home, all you have to do is switch it on or plug an appliance into an electrical outlet.

The world is full of electric energy, but most of it is in a form we cannot use. Lightning is one example of electric energy that we cannot use. We can't convert the electric energy in a flash of lightning into useful electricity. Most of the electricity we use in our homes is made by generators at power stations. These generators are really energy converters. They convert kinetic energy at the power station into electric energy. The kinetic energy is produced by burning fuel, by moving water, or by wind power.

Making your own electricity

Do you have a lamp on your bicycle? If you do, then you may have a simple type of generator called a **dynamo** that makes the lamp shine. The dynamo contains a strong magnet and a coil. When the bicycle wheels turn, the coil rotates between the poles of the magnet, and an electric current starts to flow in the coil. The dynamo converts the kinetic energy of the turning wheel into electric energy to light the lamp. You can easily see this working if you turn your bicycle upside down and turn the pedals by hand.

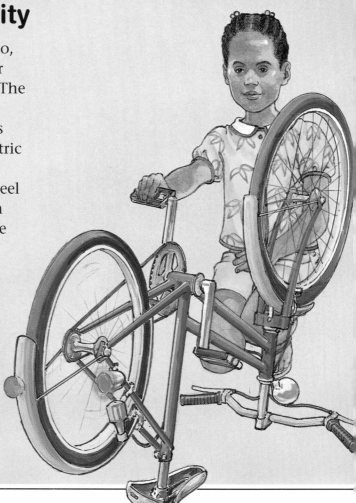

You can make electricity yourself if your bicycle has a dynamo. The generators in a power station work in much the same way as a dynamo.

What is a power pool?

One problem with electric energy from power stations is that it cannot easily be stored. Once the electric energy has been made, it must travel along the cables and wires to where it is needed. Most power stations are linked to a network of cables called a **power pool**. When there is a big demand for electricity—for example, for air conditioning during very hot weather—more power stations send electricity into the power pool. When less energy is needed, some of the power stations reduce the amount of electricity they produce. Some countries make more electricity than they need. They sell the spare energy to countries that do not have enough.

Wires carry the supply of electricity from this power station to places where it is needed.

Inside a power station

When you're traveling by train or riding along in a bus or car, you can easily spot a power station if you pass one. Many power stations have very tall towers called **cooling towers.** White clouds pour out of them. These are clouds of condensed water vapor, which is formed by steam as it mixes with cold air.

The power of steam

Power stations that burn coal or oil have three main parts—the **boiler,** the **turbines,** and the **generator.** The power station burns coal or oil to produce heat in its boiler. The boiler is lined with pipes carrying water, which boils and turns to steam. The steam is then piped to the turbines. A turbine is a series of wheels, each with many fanlike blades, mounted on a shaft. The steam rushes through the turbines and turns the steel blades.

After the steam has passed through the turbine, it enters a **condenser.** The condenser contains pipes that cool the steam, which turns back into water. This water is then pumped back to the boiler to be turned into steam again. The water in the condenser pipes is cooled in the cooling tower. The cooling tower has a series of decks. The water spills down from one deck to another, cooling as it comes into contact with the air. The cooled water is recycled through the condenser or discharged into a body of water.

Whether power stations use oil, coal, or nuclear fuel, they all produce steam that drives huge turbine wheels.

cooling tower

boiler

water droplets

cold water

Inside the generator

The central rod, or **shaft**, of the turbine is connected to a coil of wire inside the generator. This coil, or **rotor**, is pushed around as the turbine wheels rotate. It rotates inside another coil, the **stator**, which is fixed and cannot turn. The movement of the rotor inside the stator generates electric power.

Some of the heat energy produced by this coal-fired power station is used to make electric power. Most of the heat energy escapes up the tall cooling towers.

Fuel for power

Power stations need large supplies of water and fuel. They are usually built near rivers or lakes so a large supply of water is always present. Coal-fired power stations are sometimes close to coal mines so that the coal can be transported easily. Oil-fired power stations are supplied with oil by pipelines.

steam flows out

stator

shaft

rotor

transformer

steam flows in

turbine

Find out more by looking
at pages   72–73
            100–101

Nuclear power

Nuclear energy is the most powerful known form of energy in the universe. There are two ways of producing it and both ways release enormous amounts of energy. One way is to split the nucleus of an atom. This process is called **nuclear fission.** The other way is to join, or fuse, the nuclei of two atoms. This process is called **nuclear fusion**, and it is happening all the time inside the sun.

In 1938, scientists first split the nucleus of an atom. All the nuclear power stations built so far use the heat from nuclear fission to generate electricity. Scientists are still trying to find a safe way of obtaining energy from nuclear fusion. When they discover how to do this, we may have power stations fueled by nuclear fusion. Fusion would be safer and cheaper than fission for producing nuclear power.

Nuclear fission takes place when the nucleus of a uranium atom splits, releasing neutrons. The neutrons hit other atoms, causing them to split, and so on. This ongoing process is known as a chain reaction.

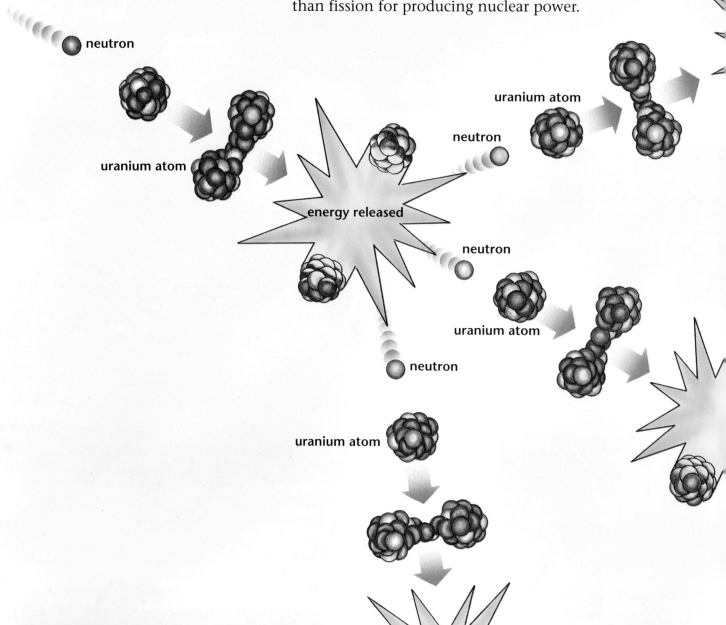

neutron

uranium atom

energy released

neutron

uranium atom

neutron

uranium atom

neutron

uranium atom

Releasing the energy

More than 425 nuclear power stations operate in the world. They produce less than 20 percent of the world's electricity.

A nuclear power station works in a similar way to an oil-fired or coal-fired power station. The difference between the two types of power stations is in the fuel they use to heat the boilers. Inside a nuclear power station, energy is released by nuclear fission in the core of a piece of equipment called the **reactor.** The energy heats water in the boiler. The water boils and produces steam. This steam turns the huge turbine wheels, and the turbines drive the generator that produces the electricity.

Nuclear fission must be carefully controlled. The fuel inside the reactor is a metal called uranium. When the nucleus of an atom of uranium is split, the neutrons released hit other atoms and split them in turn. More energy is released each time another atom splits. This is called a **chain reaction.**

Inside the reactor in a nuclear power station, the nuclei of the uranium atoms are split.

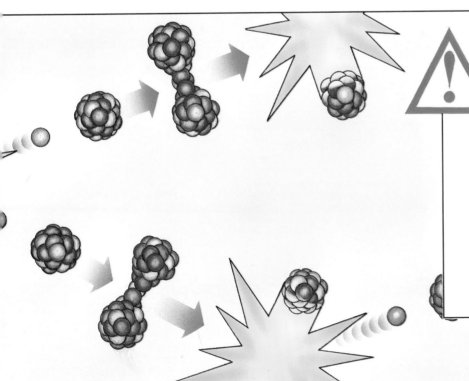

Safety first

Nuclear reactors release another kind of energy called **radioactivity.** If radioactivity escapes into the atmosphere, it can quickly cause serious damage to humans, animals, and plants. This is why a nuclear reactor is sealed inside a shield of reinforced concrete.

Hydroelectric power

Did you know that a power station can produce electricity without burning coal or oil, and without using nuclear fuel? How? A power station can turn the potential energy of water into kinetic energy and then convert this energy into electric energy by using a generator. This kind of power station is called a **hydroelectric** power station.

Water drives the wheels

Hydroelectric power stations are usually found in mountainous areas where there is plenty of rainfall. A large dam built across a river holds back a huge lake of water. Pipes carry the water downhill to a kind of waterwheel, called a water turbine, that is connected to a generator. There are two kinds of water turbines. Inside an **impulse turbine**, water flows onto the blades or paddles of a paddle-wheel and forces it to turn. In a **reaction turbine**, water flows out of jets fixed to a wheel. As the water squirts out, the wheel turns. Water turbines thus convert the energy of moving water into electric energy.

The water held by this dam has high potential energy. When the water rushes down to drive the turbines, the potential energy becomes kinetic energy.

You will need:

a modeling knife

stiff cardboard

scissors

a cork

a metal knitting needle

You will need:

scissors

a pencil

two pieces of string, about 8 inches (20 cm) and 12 inches (30 cm) long

an empty plastic bottle (a bottle made of thick plastic works best)

Make your own turbine

You can make simple models of both kinds of water turbines.

Adult supervision required!

An impulse turbine

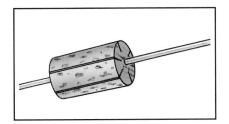

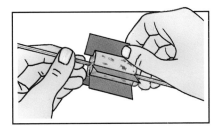

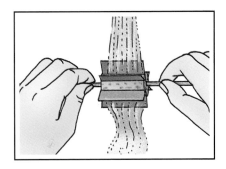

1. Push the needle carefully through the center of the cork.

2. Ask an adult to help you cut six slots round the edge of the cork. Make sure the slots are not cut right to the center of the cork.

3. Cut six paddle shapes out of the cardboard and slide one into each slot. Old photographs will also make good paddles. (Make sure you get permission before cutting up a photograph.) This is your paddle-wheel.

4. Loosely hold each end of the needle and place your paddle-wheel under a tap of cold running water. It will spin freely between your fingers.

A reaction turbine

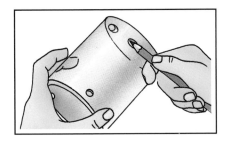

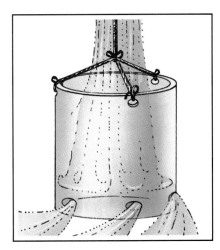

1. Ask an adult to cut the top off the plastic bottle to make a cylinder. Use your scissors to make about six to eight holes around the bottom of the cylinder.

2. Push a sharp pencil through each hole and twist the pencil to one side so that the hole is slanted. Make three small holes around the top of the cylinder.

3. Tie the short string to two of the holes in the cylinder top. Tie the long string to the third hole. Tie this to the middle of the short string but leave a long end free.

4. Hold your cylinder under the cold water tap and fill it with water. As the water flows out, it will come out sideways and cause the cylinder to spin.

Find out more by looking at pages **94–95**

Solar power

More energy reaches Earth from the sun than could be converted by millions of power stations. The sun's energy costs nothing, but how can we use it?

We can use the sun's energy to heat the water in our homes. One way this can be done is with a **flat-plate collector.** A flat-plate collector is a glass-topped box fixed to the roof of a building, facing the sun. The inside of the box is painted black. Black is best at taking in, or absorbing, heat. Water flows through pipes inside the box. During daylight, this water is heated by the sun's energy.

A flat-plate collector

You can see how a flat-plate collector works by making your own. Do this on a bright, sunny day.

You will need:

a sheet of clear plastic or glass

water

a thermometer

a black baking tray, or one that you line with black plastic

1. Fill the baking tray with cold water 1/2 inch (1.25 cm) deep. Use the thermometer to find out the water temperature. If you don't have one, test the water with your finger.

2. Place the glass or plastic over the tray. Leave it in the sunshine for an hour.

3. Take the lid off the tray and put the thermometer or your finger back into the water. What has happened to the water temperature?

This solar furnace in southern France collects enough of the sun's energy to melt metals.

Many watches and calculators are powered by solar cells. Solar cells can also power other electronic and electrical machines.

Collecting the sun's heat

Heat can be produced by using mirrors to direct and concentrate the sun's rays. One solar furnace in southern France uses a giant, curved mirror made up of smaller mirrors to collect sunlight. The mirror then directs the sun's energy onto a huge furnace. A solar power station in the Mojave Desert uses 1,800 mirrors.

Solar cells, also known as **photovoltaic cells**, are made of layers of a material that produces electric energy when light shines on it. The solar cell converts the sun's energy into electric energy. Watches and calculators can be fitted with solar cells. We say that they are solar powered, although they run on indoor lighting, too. Larger solar cells provide electric energy in places that are far from normal electricity supplies. Most artificial satellites are also powered by solar cells.

Wind power

The wind has been a source of energy for thousands of years. Before the development of the steam engine, most ships relied on wind power to fill their sails and push them along. **Windmills** were used to turn grindstones and pump water. Now scientists are turning to wind power again. This time they are using it to generate electricity.

Windmills have been used to produce electricity since the early 1900's. It is easy to produce electricity from a **wind turbine**. A wind turbine is simply a windmill that converts the kinetic energy of the wind into electricity.

Small wind turbines are used by farmers in remote parts of Australia and North America. In wide open spaces, these turbines can make some of the electricity that farmhouses need. However, the winds are sometimes so strong that they damage the turbines and put them out of action.

Engineers have designed many different kinds of wind turbines to try to solve this problem. Some turbines look like old-fashioned windmills, with four blades, or sails. Other, more modern windmills have two blades like those of an aircraft propeller.

In North America, this type of traditional windmill is used to pump water.

Wind turbine

One of the largest wind turbines in the world stands in Hawaii. It has two blades 165 feet (50 meters) long on top of a high tower. There is a smaller turbine on Orkney, off the coast of Scotland. It can generate enough electricity for about 1,000 homes. Most wind turbines are mounted on a cap, or swivel, on top of a tower. This means that they can be turned to face the wind when its direction changes.

A huge power station driven by wind has been built in the Mojave Desert in California. Its owners call it a "wind farm." Hundreds of wind turbines are arranged in rows and all are linked by wires. The electricity they produce is supplied to the California power pool.

The blades of this wind turbine in Orkney can revolve up to 34 times every minute.

These wind turbines supply electricity to homes and factories.

Power from waves and tides

This tidal power station in Brittany, France, is called the Rance Barrier.

Have you ever watched the sea during a storm? The waves crash down with enormous energy. Sometimes they are strong enough to damage seaside walls and buildings, or even make cliffs crumble. Do you know how we can make use of energy from the waves?

Rafts on the sea

One idea is to place a line of rafts floating on the sea. These rafts move up and down with the waves, and their kinetic energy can be converted to electricity. One type of raft is the Salter duck, named after its British inventor, Stephen Salter. Salter ducks bob up and down as the waves pass by. Their movement produces energy that pumps water through a turbine, which then turns a generator.

Adult supervision required!

You will need:

a piece of stiff wire, about 1 foot (30 centimeters) long

a sharp pencil

a modeling knife

a large bowl

water

five corks

beads or buttons

a knitting needle or skewer

Make your own wave energy

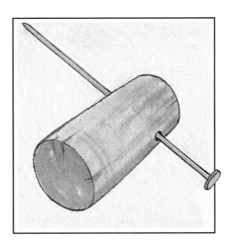

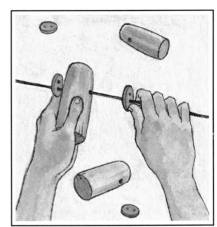

1. Ask an adult to heat a knitting needle and make a hole two-thirds of the way down each cork.

2. Thread the wire through the corks, adding a button or bead between the corks.

Tidal power

The energy in the sea's tides, which rise and fall every day, can be converted to hydroelectric power. When the tide comes in, the water is stored behind a dam. When the tide goes out, the water flows from the dam through a turbine and produces electricity. **Tidal power stations** operate in northern France, on the Annapolis River in the Canadian province of Nova Scotia, and at Murmansk, Russia.

As the tide water flows out, it passes through turbines to generate electricity. There are few large tidal power stations because they are expensive to build.

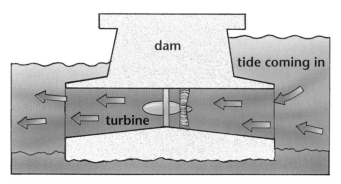

dam

tide coming in

turbine

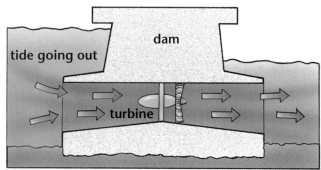

tide going out

dam

turbine

3. Check that the corks can turn freely. Bend up each end of the wire to keep the corks in place.

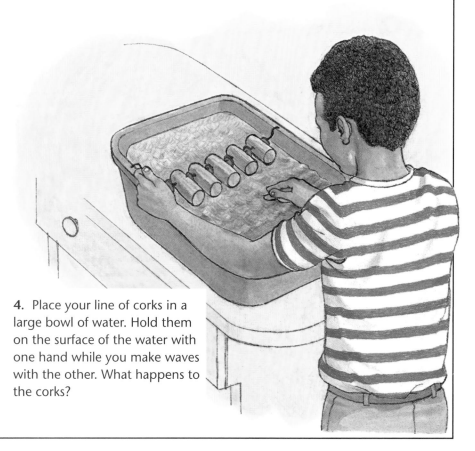

4. Place your line of corks in a large bowl of water. Hold them on the surface of the water with one hand while you make waves with the other. What happens to the corks?

Hot rocks

Do you know what it is like at the center of Earth? It is very, very hot. The temperature is thought to be about 13,000 °F (7000 °C), which is hot enough to melt rock. The heat spreads to the rock around the center of Earth and to water trapped between the layers of rock. In some parts of the world, this hot water is close to Earth's surface. By pumping it out of the ground as hot water or steam, engineers have tapped a new source of energy. This energy is called **geothermal energy**, which means it is heat energy from under the ground.

Tropical fruit grows in Iceland!

Hot water from inside Earth may be used directly to heat buildings. In Iceland, where there are many hot springs, hot water heats greenhouses and swimming pools as well as homes. And although Iceland is close to the Arctic Ocean, people living there can grow bananas and other tropical fruit in their greenhouses!

Steam condenses into white clouds of water vapor rising from these hot springs in Iceland. At least six countries have developed geothermal power plants to heat homes and generate electricity.

Making electricity

At least six countries in the world, including the United States, Iceland, Italy, and New Zealand, have built geothermal power stations. Steam coming out of the ground at high pressure is used to run steam turbines that generate electricity.

Engineers are trying to find out how more countries might use geothermal energy. They started with a question. If the rock below the surface is hot but there is no water down there, why not drill a hole through the rock, pump cold water down, and let the rock heat it up? Then the hot water could be pumped up again through a second hole.

Some engineers are working on an even better idea. They want to build a geothermal power station underground. An electric cable would then be needed to bring the electric power to the surface of Earth.

At the right of this picture, swimmers in Iceland enjoy a dip in the Blue Lagoon, an artificial lake filled by the geothermal power station in the background. The hot geothermal waste water contains salt like seawater. Geothermal power uses Earth's natural heat to generate electricity.

Find out more by looking
at pages   **66–67**
          96–97

Biomass

Have you ever lit wood to make a campfire? In some countries, people might make fires using sugar cane, cornstalks, or spoiled grain. Such organic materials that can be converted into energy or a source of energy are known as **biomass.** Dried seaweed and dried animal dung can also be used as a source of energy. Biomass is an important fuel in developing countries, where it is used for cooking and heating.

There is energy in biomass because plants and animals take in energy from the sun as they live and grow. Some forms of biomass are renewable energy sources. For example, if trees are cut down for fuel, new ones can be planted. Biomass also can be used to produce usable gases and liquid fuels. A gas called **methane** is produced naturally when biomass decays. Methane can be collected and burned to cook food, heat homes, or produce electricity.

This peat in Ireland may be burned as fuel.

Cars in Brazil can run on a fuel made from sugar cane. This is one of several fuels that are being developed as a substitute for gasoline.

Sugar cane is a crop that can be converted to alcohol and used as a fuel.

Sugar is powerful stuff

Energy can be obtained from biomass in other ways, too. One way is to make fuel for cars from sugar cane. In Brazil, most new automobiles run on a fuel made from sugar cane. Sugar cane grows easily and quickly in tropical countries. When it is fermented by using yeast and then boiled, it produces a high-energy liquid called **alcohol**. Like gasoline, the alcohol can be burned in engines.

Some gas stations in the United States sell a type of alcohol called **ethanol**, which is made with fermented grain or sugar.

Other plants, like cassava, wheat, and even seaweed, can be converted into alcohol.

Biogas

Biogas is a source of cheap energy for many villages in China. This tractor is fueled by methane, a mixture of biogas and carbon dioxide.

Dead animals and plants rot and decay. In swampy areas, for example, dead plants fall into the water. As they decay, they give off gas. Scientists call this **biogas.** Biogas comes from garbage, sewage, and manure, too.

Valuable methane

Biogas is a valuable source of energy that is often wasted. When materials decay, the biogas mixes with carbon dioxide, forming a gas called **methane**. Large amounts of methane can be dangerous—a tiny spark near the gas can cause an explosion. But if methane is collected safely and stored correctly, it can provide an important source of energy.

Making biogas

Biogas could be important in countries where other fuels are scarce or too expensive. A small village can use its own garbage and sewage to produce biogas. People collect the droppings of farm animals and put them in a tank. Some of the waste turns to liquid. The liquid soon starts to give off methane, which is kept in a storage tank that has an expandable lid. The gas can be used in homes for cooking and heating, or as fuel to power an engine or an electric generator.

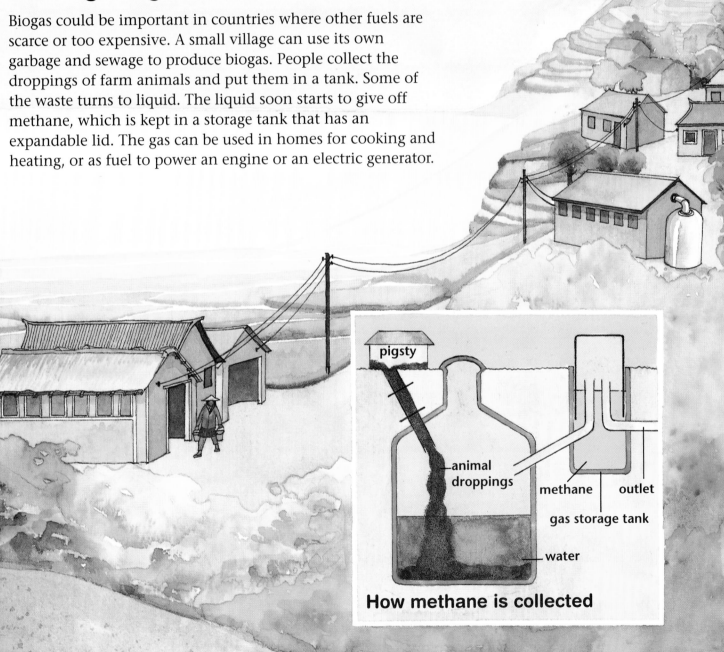

pigsty

animal droppings

methane

outlet

gas storage tank

water

How methane is collected

Amplitude: Distance between height of crest and trough of a *radio wave*.

Answering machine: Electronic device that answers the phone and records messages.

Atom: Tiny bits of matter that join to make everything we see. An atom contains a mass of protons and neutrons in a center called a nucleus that is surrounded by electrons.

Biogas: Gas given off from dead animals and plants as they decay. Biogas comes from garbage, sewage, and manure.

Biomass: Organic material, such as plants, that can be converted into energy or a source of energy. Biomass is an important fuel in developing countries.

Cable: Bundle of wires or *optical fibers* that carry pulses of energy, such as electricity or light. It is used to send messages.

Calorie: Unit that measures the amount of energy provided by food.

Coal: Black substance that forms in the earth from matter that has decayed.

Communication network: An electronic network linking cable television, telephone systems, and computer networks.

Conduction: Flow of energy through a substance.

Conductor: Material that allows energy to travel through it.

Decibel: Unit used to measure the intensity of sound.

Electromagnetic energy: Waves of energy made up of vibrations of electricity and magnetism.

Electron: Tiny particle that surrounds the nucleus of atoms. Electrons have a negative charge.

E-mail or **Electronic mail:** Message typed on a computer and sent to another computer using a *modem*.

Energy: The ability to do work.

Fax or **Facsimile:** Device that sends and receives written messages and pictures over telephone lines.

Fiber-optic communication: Communication using beams of laser light transmitted down fiber-optic cable made of very thin strands of flexible glass or plastic.

Flat-plate collector: Glass-topped box fixed to the roof of a building. The inside of the box is painted black. Water flows through pipes inside the box. During daylight, this water is heated by the sun's energy.

Fossil fuel: Energy developed from the remains of prehistoric plants and animals. Fossil fuels include coal, natural gas, and petroleum, from which we get oil.

Frequency: Rate at which something vibrates.

Geothermal energy: Energy that is produced wherever water comes into contact with heated underground rocks and turns into steam.

Glucose: One of the main sugars from which living things get energy.

HDTV: High-definition television, a television system that provides a sharper image on a wider screen.

Hydroelectric power: Energy that comes from falling water.

Inertia: Basic characteristic of an object. Inertia makes an object that is not moving remain motionless unless some force puts it into motion. It also makes a moving object continue to move at a constant speed and in the same direction unless some outside force changes the object's motion.

Integrated circuit: Very small, thin chip of silicon containing all the elements of a circuit: diodes, capacitors, resistors, and transistors.

Internet: A global network of computer networks.

Kinetic energy: Energy of movement.

Laser: Machine that produces a concentrated beam of light. Lasers are used in medicine and industry.

Microwave: Form of energy. A microwave is a superhigh frequency *radio wave*.

Mobile telephone: Telephone that uses radio waves to send and receive.

Modem: Electronic device (short for modulator/demodulator) that converts a computer's digital signals into sound signals for transmission over a telephone line, and converts the sound signals back into digital signals.

Molecule: Smallest unit remaining when a substance has been divided as much as possible without having undergone a chemical change.

Neutron: Tiny particle found in the nucleus of atoms. Neutrons have no electric charge.

Nuclear fission: Splitting of the *nucleus* of an atom into two nearly equal parts.

Nuclear fusion: Process by which two nuclei combine and form a *nucleus* of a heavier element.

Nucleus: Center of an atom. A nucleus is made of tiny particles called *protons* and *neutrons.*

Optical fiber: Glass or plastic fiber so thin it can be threaded through the eye of a needle.

Pager: Small, handheld device that receives a radio signal and displays a short message.

Photovoltaic cell: Object made of layers of material that produces electric energy when light shines on it. A photovoltaic cell converts the sun's energy into electric energy.

Potential energy: Energy that is stored and waiting to be used.

Protein: Food substance necessary for the growth and maintenance of body structures.

Proton: Tiny particle found in the *nucleus* of atoms. Protons have a positive electric charge.

Radioactive: Giving off energy as a result of decay of the nucleus of an atom.

Reactor: Piece of equipment in which energy is released by *nuclear fission.* A reactor is found in a nuclear power plant.

Semiconductor: A material that only conducts electricity in certain ways; used in transistors.

Solar cell: Energy converter that converts light energy from the sun into electric energy.

Solar energy: Energy from the light of the sun.

Sound waves: Vibrations that can be heard.

Telecommunications: The sending of information across a distance by means of electronic devices.

Telegram: Message sent by telegraph.

Telegraph: Instrument for sending messages over long distances. It includes a key, which is used to send a message, and a sounder, which receives the message.

Transistor: Instrument that controls the flow of an electric current inside a radio, computer, or other electronic device.

Transmitter: Device used to send messages.

Ultraviolet ray: Invisible form of light. Ultraviolet rays come from the sun along with visible light.

Vibration: Continuous back-and-forth movement.

Videophone: Telephone with a small television camera and screen, used to transmit and receive calls with both video and sound signals.

Voice mail or **Voice messaging system:** Computerized automated answering system used to answer phones and record messages.

Wavelength: Distance between the peak of one wave and the peak of a wave that is next to it.

Wave, radio: Electromagnetic wave that is used to carry information through the air and outer space.

Wave, sound: Vibration in the air that makes noise.

World Wide Web (WWW): A service provided through the Internet, allowing computer users to "see" pages of material on distant computers.

Acknowledgements

The publishers of **World Book's** *Young Scientist* acknowledge the following photographers, publishers, agencies, and corporations for photographs used in this volume.

Cover © M. L. Sinbaldi, The Stock Market; Intelsat; NASA

2/3 NASA

8/9 © Stewart Cohen, Stone

16/17 Corbis/Bettmann

20/21 Brown Brothers

22/23 Brown Brothers; © Alan Schein, The Stock Market; Janet Heintz © *Chicago Tribune*; WORLD BOOK photo by Steven Spicer

32/33 Mary Evans Picture Library; TyCom Ltd.

38/39 © Bill Aron, PhotoEdit; © David R. Frazier

42/43 © Nelson Morris, Science Photo Library; © Astrid & Hans Frieder, Science Photo Library; Corbis/Bettmann

44/45 Hewlett Packard; © Nintendo (WORLD BOOK photo by Jeff Guerrant); © James Holmes/SPL from Photo Researchers

46/47 © Jeff Zaruba, The Stock Market

50/51 Intelsat

52/53 © David R. Frazier; © Larry Mulvehill/SPL from Photo Researchers

56/57 © Phillip Hayson, Photo Researchers; © David Parker, Science Photo Library

58/59 AT&T; Zenith Electronics Corporation

60/61 © Gary D. Landsman, The Stock Market

66/67 © Robert Harding Picture Library

68/69 © Photri from Robert Harding Picture Library; © M. Mehltretter, ZEFA Picture Library

70/71 © ZEFA Picture Library

72–75 © Robert Harding Picture Library

76/77 © Lori Adamski-Peek, Stone; Apple Color Photography

80/81 © Bruce Coleman Collection

82/83 © ZEFA Picture Library

84/85 © Xinhue News from ZEFA Picture Library

86/87 © Jonathon T. Wright, Bruce Coleman Collection

88/89 © U.W.S. from ZEFA Picture Library

90/91 © J. Lepore, ZEFA Picture Library

92/93 Kenetech Corporation; © D. Ball, Spectrum Colour Library

94/95 © V-Dia Verlag, ZEFA Picture Library

96/97 © John Cancalosi, Bruce Coleman Collection; © G. Fleming, Frank Lane Picture Agency

98–101 © Streichan, ZEFA Picture Library

102/103 © Bramaz, ZEFA Picture Library

104/105 © Sherman, ZEFA Picture Library

106/107 © ZEFA Picture Library

108/109 © Michael Marten, Science Photo Library; © T. Braise, ZEFA Picture Library

110/111 © J. Pfaff, ZEFA Picture Library

112/113 © Spectrum Colour Library; © Bernard Edmaier/SPL from Photo Researchers

114/115 © Farrell Grehan, Photo Researchers; © D. F. E. Russel, Robert Harding Picture Library; © ZEFA Picture Library

Illustrated by

Martin Aitchinson
Nigel Alexander
Hemesh Alles
Martyn Andrews
Sue Barclay
Richard Berridge
John Booth
Lou Bory
Maggie Brand
Stephen Brayfield
Bristol Illustrators
Colin Brown
Estelle Carol
David Cook
Marie DeJohn
Richard Deverell
Farley, White and Veal
Sheila Galbraith
Peter Geissler
Jeremy Gower
Kathie Kelleher
Stuart Lafford

John Lobban
Louise Martin
Annabel Milne
Yoshi Miyake
Donald Moss
Eileen Mueller Neill
Teresa O'Brien
Paul Perreault
Roberta Polfus
Jeremy Pyke
Trevor Ridley
Barry Rowe
Don Simpson
Gary Slater
Lawrie Taylor
Gwen Tourret
Pat Tourret
Peter Visscher
David Webb
Gerald Whitcomb
Matthew White
Lynne Willey